QUILTED
CURVES
& STRIPS

GO! Baby™ Friendly

With the AccuQuilt GO!®

Edited by Carolyn S. Vagts

HOUSE of
WHITE
BIRCHES

PUBLISHERS
SINCE 1947

Table of Contents

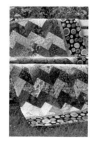

Introduction

These days, many busy quilters are looking to save time, use up stash fabrics and still create a stylish, one-of-a-kind masterpiece quilt. For the most part, quilting techniques stay the same, but there are a few new and exciting tools and techniques to help make the process quicker and much easier.

A talented group of designers were given the opportunity to play with the AccuQuilt GO!® and GO! Baby™. The results were astounding. In this book you will see great designs created with AccuQuilt GO! and the GO! Baby. These quilts will inspire you to try something a bit different, sort of a new twist on traditional piecing. Designs will take you on a journey in a totally different direction and give you the time-saving options you have secretly been looking for. No longer will you have to sacrifice design because you don't have the time. The AccuQuilt system makes curved piecing a snap and the designers will show you how. No more long hours tracing templates and cutting them out. With the AccuQuilt system, it's fast and you get perfect pieces every time.

General Instructions

These general instructions are intended as guidelines for the cutting and construction techniques used in all of the quilt patterns in this book. Refer to these general instructions or the materials that came with your cutter for guidance on using your machine.

Most projects in *Quilted Curves & Strips with AccuQuilt GO!®* are made with a selection of shapes that can be used on both the AccuQuilt GO! and GO! Baby™ fabric-cutting systems. Both systems feature precise, quick cutting with safety. The GO! Baby is compatible with more than 60 percent of the GO! dies. The AccuQuilt die shapes used in this book are listed in the Fabric Reference Chart on page 5. Check individual pattern materials lists for the specific die used in each pattern and whether that die is compatible with the AccuQuilt

GO! and/or GO! Baby. For even more information on the dies, go to accuquilt.com and enter the individual die number. Don't worry if you do not own the strip cutters. Instead, cut the number of strips needed with a rotary cutter and cutting mat.

Let's get started!

Tip

Look for handy cutting and construction tips throughout this book to help make your GO! quilts a success.

Using Your AccuQuilt GO! Cutter

To use the AccuQuilt cutters, first precut appropriately sized strips to feed through the cutter. These strips can be layered or fan-folded to cut multiple shapes in one pass. The Fabric Reference Chart on page 5 shows precut strip sizes, fan-fold widths, number of shapes (cuts) that can be made from one fabric strip length and the approximate number of shapes that can be made from a single yard of fabric for the die shapes used in this book.

The GO! and GO! Baby cutters can cut up to six layers of cotton quilting fabric at a time. However, it is suggested that you begin with fewer fabric layers and build up with increased skill and experience to avoid jamming the machine. Even the same type of fabric is not always the same thickness. The properties of quilting cotton can vary from brand to brand. For best results, use the cutter on a flat, hard, clean surface so the rubber feet can grip and hold the cutter in place. If the machine lifts while cutting, you might be cutting too many layers or the material is not suitable for cutting. Remove a layer and try again.

> ### Tip
> *Take care of your cutting mats. Store mats flat, out of direct sunlight and heat. Do not use a warped mat. Alternate mat sides when cutting to extend cutting life. Replace mats when cutting performance of dies is reduced or mat shows excessive wear.*

Use a mat that matches the size of die board being used. Cut with die blades running under the roller at an angle, not parallel to the roller, if possible. Align fabric to the edge of the shape being cut, not the edge of the die board. Refer to your GO! user's manual for other tips and care and maintenance of the cutter and dies.

Be sure to read the entire user's manual before using your cutter. Never carry the GO! cutter in open position.

> ### Tip
> *Test-cut one shape before cutting many shapes to ensure fabric orientation is correct.*

For questions about your AccuQuilt GO! Fabric Cutter, refer to your user's manual or contact AccuQuilt Customer Service at (888) 258-7913 or online at accuquilt.com.

1 Place die on cutter, FOAM SIDE UP. Place fabric on top of die. **Note:** *To conserve fabric, cover only the shape you want to cut—not the entire die board. For asymmetrical shapes, place fabric pattern side up if you want the shape to look exactly like the shape on the die. Place fabric pattern side down if you want the shape to be a mirror image of the shape on the die. Place cutting mat on top of fabric.*

2 Push die, fabric and mat firmly against roller. Turn handle in direction you want the die to go.

3 Remove mat, die-cut shape and excess fabric. Add new fabric and cutting mat on top of die. Repeat process from opposite side. There is no need to handle the die between cuts!

Fabric Reference Chart

Use this chart to determine the minimum fabric requirements needed to cut each GO!® fabric-cutting die shape listed.

Die Name (Item #)	Shape on Die	Layers of Cotton Fabric*	Precut Strip Size (width of fabric)	Fan-Fold Size	Cuts Per Precut Strip	Minimum Shapes Yielded Per 40" Usable-Width Yard Fabric	Helpful Hints
Geometric Shapes							
GO! Square—6½" (55000)	Square	Up to 6	7½"	7½"	5	20	
GO! Square—3½" (55006)	Squares	Up to 6	8"	4½"	16	72 or more	
GO! Half Square—3" Finished Triangle (55009)	Half-Square Triangles	Up to 6	9½"	4½"	32 or more	128	For easy half-square triangles, layer fabrics right sides together on die and cut. Pick up one pair of triangles and sew.
GO! Half Square—4" Finished Triangle (55031)	Half-Square Triangles	Up to 6	11½"	5½"	28	84	For easy half-square triangles, layer fabrics right sides together on die and cut. Pick up one pair of triangles and sew.
Value Die (55018) Die set includes 4½" Square, 2½" Square and Half Square—2" Finished Triangles	Half-Square—2" Finished Triangles	Up to 6	3"	4"	20	240	For easy half-square triangles, layer fabrics right sides together on die and cut. Pick up one pair of triangles and sew.
GO! Rectangle—3½" W x 6½" H (55005)	Rectangle	Up to 6	7½"	4½"	8	32 or more	
Strip Cutter							
GO! Strip Cutter—2½" (55014)	Strips	Up to 6	8½" (for 3 strips), 25½" (for 9 strips)	8½"	3 per 8½"	12	Position fabric on die so folded edge goes through first.
GO! Strip Cutter—3½" (55032)	Strips	Up to 6	8" (for 2 strips), 24" (for 6 strips)	8"	2 per 8"	9	Position fabric on die so folded edge goes through first.
Classic Shapes							
GO! Double Wedding Ring (2-Die Set) (55078)	Center Shape	Up to 6	10"	10"	4	12	
	Corner Shape	Up to 6	3½"	3½"	11	110	
	Oval (Melon) Shape	Up to 6	7½"	3"	13	52	
	Middle Arc Shape	Up to 6	3½"	3½"	11	110	
	Arc Shape	Up to 6	3½"	3½"	11	110	
	Total Arc Shape	Up to 6	10"	4½"	8	24	
GO! Rob Peter to Pay Paul (2-Die Set) (55068)	Block Center	Up to 6	9"	9"	4	16	
	Block Edge	Up to 6	9"	6"	12	48	
GO! Tumbler—3½" (55015)	Tumblers	Up to 6	11½"	4½"	24	72 or more	
GO! Winding Ways (55069)	A, B and C Shapes	Up to 6	10"	8½"	8 out of each shape	24 of each shape	Align lengthwise grain of fabric with straight blades on die.
GO! Drunkard's Path—3½" Finished (55070)	Arc shape and Quarter Circle	Up to 6	11"	6"	12 sets	36 sets	3½" finished size, creates 7" finished block.
GO! Chisels (55039)	Chisels	Up to 6	11"	4½"	16	48	Layer fabric all wrong sides up or down to cut chisels in the same direction. Place fabric on die right sides together to cut pairs.
GO! Apple Core—6¼" Finished (55036)	Apple Core	Up to 6	8"	6½"	6	24 or more	

*Recommended layers of fabric are based on 100 percent cotton fabric. Number of layers of fabric varies by fabric type and thickness. Always begin with fewer layers and build up.

Fabric Guide for GO!

Fabric Type	Number of Layers*
Batik	Up to 6; up to 4 prefused
Cotton	Up to 6; up to 4 prefused
Denim	1
Felt	1
Flannel	Up to 2
Fleece	Up to 2
Ultrasuede	1
Wool	2

*Recommended Cutting Layers: The AccuQuilt GO!® Fabric Cutter cuts a wide variety of fabric in a varying number of layers. The number of layers you can cut depends on the type of material and the intricacy of the die. Always begin with fewer layers, and then build up. Often, more layers will improve cutting performance.

Basic Quilt Making Techniques

Begin any quilting project by reading through all instructions. Like cooking, knowing what prep work needs to be done and gathering all the necessary "ingredients and tools" prior to starting will make your quilting experience better.

There are several tools that every quilter needs in their sewing box (besides the AccuQuilt cutter and a sewing machine). Basics include:

• Seam ripper

• Pincushion

• Hand-sewing needles and long, thin, sharp pins

• Measuring tools

• Fabric marking tools for dark and light fabrics

• Fabric scissors

• Iron and ironing surface

• Sewing machine needles sizes 75/11–80/12

• Ergonomic rotary cutter and at least an 18" self-healing cutting mat and 6" x 24" see-through quilting ruler

Pre-washing fabrics is a personal choice. Some quilting cottons will shrink more and contain more residual dye than others. If washing, launder all fabrics you will be using. Don't mix washed and unwashed fabrics. Iron all fabrics before cutting.

Straighten your fabric yardage before doing any cutting. This will help you keep your fabric on grain when cutting. For best results when using the AccuQuilt cutter, try to lay fabrics on the die with the straight grain along a shape edge. Your fabric will cut better and the pieces will retain their shape while being sewn.

All projects in this book assume piecing with a ¼"-wide seam, sewn right sides together. Good pressing at each stage of block construction makes for a beautiful project. Set stitches by pressing seams flat. Specific pressing instructions will be noted in each pattern.

Finishing Your Quilt

After piecing the quilt top as instructed, finish your project with these easy steps:

1. Mark quilting designs on the quilt top before layering with the batting and backing by tracing with a washable marking tool, using perforated paper patterns and chalk or purchased tear-away paper patterns. Some quilting designs—like meandering or stippling, outline or stitch-in-the-ditch—do not require marking.

2. After ironing the backing, place it right side down on a clean, flat surface. For large projects, tape the edges of the backing to the floor or table using low adhesive painter's tape, pulling it taut.

3. Place the batting on top of the backing, centering on the backing and smoothing out wrinkles.

4. Fold the quilt top in half lengthwise, right sides together, and lay centered on the batting. Unfold the quilt top and smooth over the batting (Figure 1). The batting and backing layers should be 3" to 8" larger than the quilt top, depending on the project's overall size.

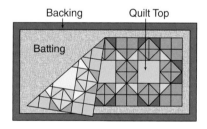

Figure 1

5. Baste the quilt layers together to prevent shifting during quilting. Hand, safety-pin or spray-baste the quilt sandwich. Hand-baste, starting in the center and moving toward the outside edge using contrasting thread. If using a spray-basting product, consult the manufacturer's directions.

6. Quilt as desired by hand or machine; remove pins or basting thread if used. Trim excess backing and batting even with quilt top.

7. When quilting is completed, binding finishes and protects the quilt edges. The following instructions are for attaching a double-fold (also called a French fold) binding with mitered corners.

Binding Edges

1. Overlap binding strips at right angles, right sides together. Sew across the diagonal and trim seam allowance to ¼", as seen in Figure 2. Press seams open. Join strips to make a length equal to the circumference of the quilt plus at least 10".

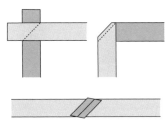

Figure 2

2. Fold ¼" to ½" of one end of the binding to the wrong side and press. Referring to Figure 3, fold the strip in half lengthwise, wrong sides together, and press again.

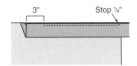

Figure 3

3. Position the turned end of binding at least 12" from a corner. Then, matching raw edges of quilt top and binding, begin stitching binding to quilt top approximately 3" from the binding end, using a ¼" seam allowance (Figure 4). *Note: To have a filled binding that will wear well and look good, use a seam allowance that is approximately half the width of the folded binding. For example, for a binding cut 2½" wide and folded to 1¼" wide, use a seam allowance ½" to ⅝".*

Figure 4

4. Sew binding to within ¼" (or your seam allowance) of the first corner; remove quilt from machine and trim threads. Fold the binding up at a 45-degree angle to the seam (Figure 5) and back down even with the quilt edges, forming a pleat at the corner (Figure 6). Resume stitching from corner through the pleat, and stitching binding to the quilt top, sewing remaining corners as above.

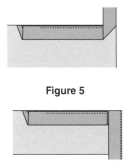

Figure 5

Figure 6

5. Stop sewing binding a short distance from the beginning tail of the binding. Remove the quilt from sewing machine and trim the end tail of the binding so that it tucks inside the beginning tail of the binding at least 2" (Figure 7). Resume stitching, sewing the binding tails to the quilt top, again referring to Figure 6.

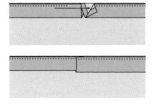

Figure 7

6. Turning binding to quilt back pulling over the seam line, stitch in place by hand or machine. Stitch a few stitches by hand in corners to close miters. ❖

Picket Fence Place Mats

Designed & Quilted by Connie Kauffman

Put a little touch of a flower garden on your table.

Project Notes

Materials listed and instructions are for two place mats.

The die chosen for this project is compatible with both the AccuQuilt GO!® and GO! Baby™ fabric-cutting systems. Refer to the die-cutting general instructions on page 4 for specific die-cutting processes.

Project Specifications

Skill Level: Beginner
Place Mat Size: 16 x 12¼"

Materials

- ¼ yard total variety floral print scraps
- ⅝ yard blue solid
- 1 yard white tone-on-tone
- Backing (2) 20" x 16"
- Batting (2) 20" x 16"
- Neutral-colored all-purpose thread
- White quilting thread
- AccuQuilt GO! Baby Fabric Cutter
- AccuQuilt GO! Chisels die (55039)
- Basic quilting tools and supplies

Die-Cutting Instructions

1. Cut one 10" x 24" blue solid rectangle; subcut four 5" x 12" rectangles. Stack rectangles right side up and die-cut eight A Chisel shapes.

2. Cut two 5" by fabric width white strips; subcut four 5" x 12" rectangles. Stack rectangles right side up and die-cut eight B Chisel shapes.

Additional Cutting Instructions

1. Cut a total of 35 (1½") floral print G squares.

2. Cut three 1½" by fabric width strip from blue solid; subcut (14) 1½" x 6½" I strips.

3. Cut three 1¾" by fabric width strips from white solid; subcut eight each 1¾" x 4" E strips and 1¾" x 5½" F strips.

4. Cut two 1½" by fabric width strips from white solid; subcut 28 (1½") H squares.

Completing the Place Mats

1. Join an A and B chisel shape along angled edges as shown in Figure 1. Repeat to make four A-B rectangles.

Make 4

A

B

Figure 1

2. Cut A-B rectangles in half lengthwise to make four each 1½" wide C and D strips (Figure 2).

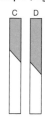

C   D

Figure 2

3. Join E to the white end of C, and F to the white end of D (Figure 3). Repeat to make four each C-E and D-F units.

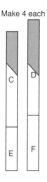

Make 4 each

C   D

E   F

Figure 3

4. Sew five G, two H and one I together as shown in Figure 4, arranging floral G squares as desired. Repeat to make seven I-G-H units.

Make 7

Figure 4

5. Arrange C-E and D-F units alternately with I-G-H units beginning with a C-E unit and ending with a D-F unit as shown in Figure 5.

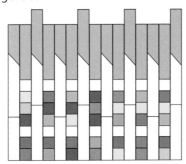

Figure 5

6. Keeping the bottom edges even, stitch the units together. Trim D-F units even with the top of the place mat.

7. Repeat steps 1–6 to make second place mat.

8. Layer batting, backing with right side up and place mat top with right side down; pin together to hold in place. Round off place mat corners by tracing around a thread spool placed in each corner. Trim corners.

9. Stitch place mat layers together ¼" from raw edge, leaving a 3" opening along one long side.

10. Clip rounded corner seam allowance and turn right side out through opening. Press edges flat. Turn opening to inside and hand-stitch closed.

11. Quilt as desired referring to Finishing Your Quilt on page 6 in General Instructions. ❖

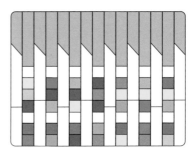

Picket Fence Place Mat
Placement Diagram 16" x 12¼"

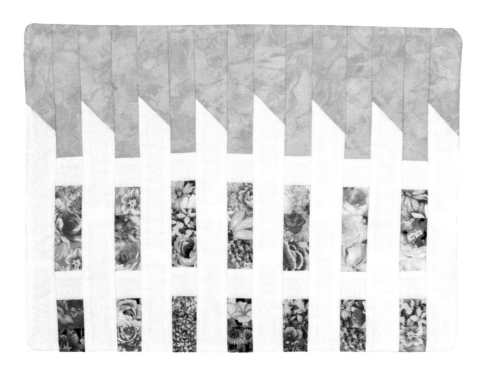

Tumbler Tote

Design by Julie Weaver

This roomy tote is a great project to use up scraps, and the Accuquilt GO! Baby Fabric Cutter makes cutting those scraps a breeze! You can tailor the size of the inside pockets to fit your personal needs. Make a tote to carry everything you need for the office, your quilt class, the pool or for Baby.

Project Note

The die chosen for this project is compatible with both the AccuQuilt GO!® and GO! Baby™ fabric-cutting systems. Refer to the die-cutting general instructions on page 4 for specific die-cutting processes.

Project Specifications

Skill Level: Confident Beginner
Tote Size: 14" x 12" x 6"

Materials

- ¼ yard floral print
- ⅝ yard white print
- 1¼ yards blue plaid
- 2 yards assorted bright prints (scraps or purchased)
- 1⅞ yard fusible fleece
- ¾" metal snap closure
- Four 2" D-rings
- Water-soluble fabric marker
- Thread to match fabrics
- Accuquilt GO! Baby Fabric Cutter
- Accuquilt GO! Tumbler Block die (55015)
- Basic sewing supplies and tools

Die-Cutting Instructions

If using assorted print scraps:
1. Sort scraps by size. Scraps at least 4½" square can be used to die-cut one Tumbler block. Scraps 4½" x 11½" can be used to die-cut three tumbler shapes. Die cut a total of 138 Tumbler shapes.

2. Stack similar-size scraps up to six layers, right sides up, or cut smaller scraps individually, referring to General Instructions for more cutting tips.

If using assorted print fabric width purchased yardage:
1. Cut six 11½" by fabric width strips and fan-fold 4½" wide.

2. Die-cut a total of 138 Tumbler blocks.

Additional Cutting Instructions

1. Cut four 5" by fabric width blue plaid B/C strips; subcut four 17" C straps and two 30" B handles.

2. Cut one 9½" by fabric width blue plaid strip; subcut two 18½" G rectangles.

3. Cut one 8½" by fabric width blue plaid strip; subcut two 9" E rectangles and one 2½" x fabric width binding strip.

4. Cut one 17½" by fabric width white print strip; subcut two 18½" D rectangles for lining.

5. Cut one 7½" by fabric width floral print strip; subcut two 18½" F rectangles.

6. From fusible fleece, cut two 17½" by fabric width strips; subcut four 18½" rectangles for tote body and lining. Cut one 7½" by fabric width strips; subcut two 7½" squares for outside pockets. Cut one 8" by fabric width strip; subcut two 18½" rectangles for inside pockets. Cut six 1¾"x fabric width strips; subcut four 15" and two 28" strips for straps and handles.

Completing Outer Tote Sides

1. Arrange and sew nine A Tumbler blocks into a row. Repeat to make six rows. Sew the rows together to make a pieced tote front as shown in Figure 1. Repeat to make a pieced tote back.

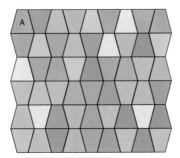

Figure 1

2. Arrange and sew five A tumbler blocks into a row. Repeat to make three rows. Sew the rows together to make an outside pocket as shown in Figure 2. Repeat to make a second outside pocket.

Figure 2

3. Measure 1" from the second vertical row of Tumbler block points on one side of the pieced tote front referring to Figure 3; trim. Repeat on opposite side to make an 18½" x 17½" pieced tote front rectangle.

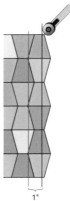

1"

Figure 3

4. Repeat step 3 to trim the pieced tote back, again referring to Figure 3.

5. Fuse front and back pieced tote rectangles to matching-size fusible fleece rectangles, following manufacturer's instructions. Quilt as desired.

6. On pieced outside pocket, measure 4½" from the center of the middle Tumbler block row referring to Figure 4 and trim each side of the pocket to make a 9" x 7½" rectangle. Repeat on second outside pocket.

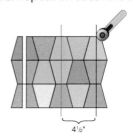

4½"

Figure 4

7. To complete one outside pocket, sew 9" edges of one E and one outside pocket right sides together. Press seam toward E. Turn right side out and match raw edges of E and outside pocket; press to make a ½" cuff at pocket top as shown in Figure 5.

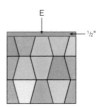

E

½"

Figure 5

8. Fuse a fusible fleece 7½" square between E and pieced outside pocket, following manufacturer's instructions. Quilt as desired to complete outside pocket.

9. Repeat steps 7 and 8 to make second outside pocket.

10. Measure 4" up from the bottom of the pieced tote front and use a washable fabric marker to draw a line across the width (Figure 6). Draw a line on outside pocket lining (E) ¼" up from bottom of pocket.

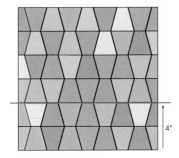

Figure 6

11. With right sides together, center outside pocket on pieced tote front matching drawn lines on pocket and pieced tote front (Figure 7). Sew on the drawn line across pocket. Flip up pocket toward top of tote and press; pin in place as shown in Figure 8.

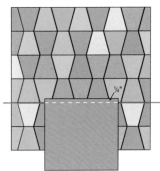

Figure 7

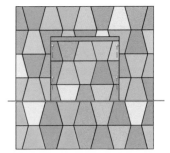

Figure 8

12. Repeat steps 10 and 11 to sew second pocket on pieced tote back.

Completing Tote Straps & Handles

1. To make one tote strap, fold and press one short end and one long side of C ¼" to wrong side. Center and fuse a 1¾" x 15" fusible fleece strip to the wrong side of C (Figure 9).

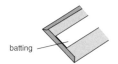

batting

Figure 9

2. Fold and press the long raw edge of C over the fleece. Then, fold and press the long pressed edge of C over the raw edge. Stitch twice along center fold and edgestitch around all edges as shown in Figure 10.

a

b

Figure 10

3. Wrap C folded short end around straight side of D-ring about 1¼", wrong sides together, and sew across strap close to C end (Figure 11).

1¼"

Figure 11

4. Repeat steps 1–3 to make four C straps.

5. Referring to Figure 12, position and pin two C straps, with D-rings at top, 3¾" from each side and 2¼" down from top of pieced tote front, covering pocket raw edges. Edgestitch long edges through all thicknesses. Repeat with remaining C straps on pieced tote back.

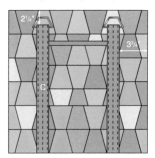

2¼"

3¾"

C

Figure 12

6. Using B strips and 1¾" x 28" fusible fleece strips to make handles, repeat steps 1 and 2, except fold both short ends of B to the wrong side.

7. Thread ends of B through D rings on pieced tote front and stitch referring to step 3 and Figure 11.

8. Repeat steps 6 and 7 for pieced tote back handle.

Completing the Outer Tote

1. With right sides together and handles pulled up out of the way, sew pieced tote front and back side seams and bottom seams together.

2. Box tote bottom by matching side and bottom seams right sides together. Stitch 3½" from corner and trim seam to ¼" (Figure 13). Repeat on opposite corner.

Figure 13

3. Turn tote right side out.

Completing the Lining

1. Fuse D to matching-size fusible fleece and quilt as desired. Repeat with second D.

2. Follow manufacturer's instructions and attach magnetic snap closure centered and 1" down from top edge to each lining piece.

3. To make one inside pocket, join G and F along both 18½" sides. Press seams toward F. Turn right side out and match raw edges of F and G; press to make a ½" cuff at pocket top as shown in Figure 14.

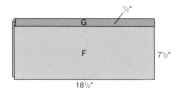

Figure 14

4. Fuse an 8" x 18½" fusible fleece piece between G and F, and quilt as desired. Repeat to make a second inside pocket.

5. Referring to steps 10–12 of Completing Outer Tote Sides, attach inside pockets to right side of front and back lining pieces (quilted D).

6. Referring to Figure 15, draw a vertical line on the inside pocket 9¼" from one side. Draw two more lines 5" on either side of the first line as shown in Figure 15.

Sew on the drawn lines to make pocket sections. Repeat on the other inside pocket. *Note: How many pocket sections you make should be determined by the intended use of the tote. This stitching arrangement will make four pocket sections on either side of the tote. Change the section sizes as desired.*

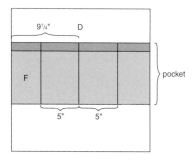

Figure 15

6. With right sides together, sew the lining front to the lining back leaving the top open. Box the bottom referring to step 2 of Completing the Outer Tote. Do not turn right side out.

Completing the Tote

1. Place the lining inside the outer tote, matching side seams and top edges. Making sure handles are pulled down and away from tote top, baste tote and lining together ⅛" from edge all around top edge.

2. Fold and press the 2½"-wide blue plaid binding strip wrong sides together. Sew the binding to the outer side of the tote using a ⅜" seam and matching raw edge of binding to raw edge of tote top.

3. Turn binding toward lining side and hand-stitch in place to finish. ❖

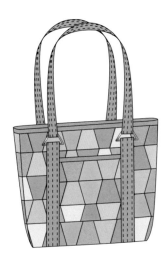

Tumbler Tote
Placement Diagram 14" x 12" x 6"

Christmas Candy Apples

Designed & Quilted by Sandra L. Hatch

Add a little cheer to your holiday table setting this year with this very creative technique. Or … change the fabrics to suit any season.

Project Note

The die chosen for this project is compatible with both the AccuQuilt GO!® and GO! Baby™ fabric-cutting systems. Refer to the die-cutting general instructions on page 4 for specific die-cutting processes.

Project Specifications

- Skill Level: Intermediate
- Runner Size: 43¼" x 15½"
- Block Size: 6¼" x 4½"
- Number of Blocks: 27

White Candy Apple
6¼" x 4½" Block
Make 13

Red Candy Apple
6¼" x 4½" Block
Make 14

Materials

- 24 assorted 1½" x 21" C strips coordinating holiday prints
- ⅝ yard green holiday print
- ⅞ yard white holiday print
- ⅞ yard red holiday print
- Batting 52" x 23"
- Backing 52" x 23"
- Neutral-color all-purpose thread
- Quilting thread
- AccuQuilt GO! Baby Fabric Cutter
- AccuQuilt GO! die: Apple Core 6¼" (55036)
- Basic quilting tools and supplies

Cutting Instructions

1. Cut three 8½" by fabric width strips white holiday print; subcut strips into (26) 4" A rectangles.

2. Cut three 8½" by fabric width strips red holiday print; subcut strips into (28) 4" B rectangles.

3. Cut 2¼" bias strips green holiday print to total 160" when joined for bias binding. ***Note:*** *Binding must be made from bias strips because of the curved outer edges of the runner.*

Piecing & Die-Cutting A-C & B-C Units

1. Select eight different C strips and join along the 21" length to make a strip set; press seams in one direction. Repeat to make a total of three C strip sets.

2. Subcut the C strip sets made in step 1 into (27) 1½" C units referring to Figure 1.

Figure 1

3. Select one C unit and sew an A rectangle to each long side to make an A-C unit as shown in Figure 2; press seams toward A. Repeat to make a total of 13 A-C units.

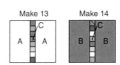

Figure 2

4. Repeat step 3 with the remaining C units and the B rectangles to make 14 B-C units, again referring to Figure 2.

5. Select and layer three A-C units on the cutter, varying the position of the strips and die-cut the shapes. Repeat with all A-C and B-C units to make a total of 13 A-C and

14 B-C apple core units as shown in Figure 3. *Note: If you would like more variety in the apple core units, die-cut the A-C and B-C units individually.*

Figure 3

Completing the Runner

1. Carefully sew the narrow convex curved end of a B-C unit into the wider concave side of an A-C unit, matching and pinning at center notches and ends and generously between as shown in Figure 4.

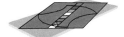

Figure 4

2. Repeat step 1, adding units to make a row containing four A-C and five B-C units as shown in Figure 5; press seams toward the concave side of the units. Repeat to make two rows.

Make 2

Figure 5

3. Repeat step 2 to make one row with five A-C units and four B-C units as shown in Figure 6.

Make 1

Figure 6

4. Join the rows referring to the Placement Diagram for positioning; press seams in one direction.

5. Layer, quilt and bind with 2¼"-wide green holiday print bias strips, following Finishing Your Quilt on page 6 of the General Instructions. ❖

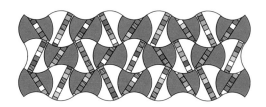

Christmas Candy Apples
Placement Diagram 43¼" x 15½"

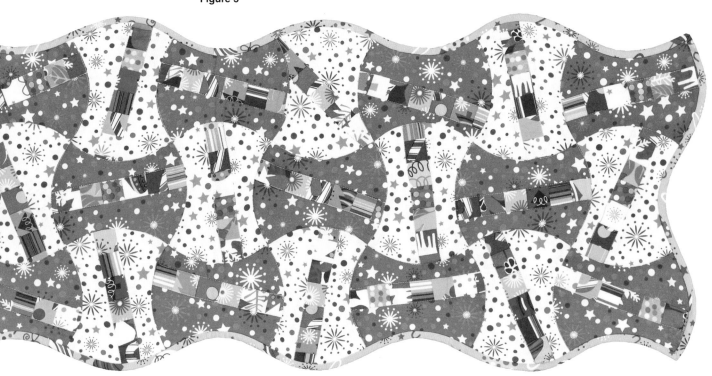

Double Wedding Ring Bed Runner

Designed & Quilted by Chris Malone

The die-cut pieces make this difficult pattern a breeze to cut.
Take a traditional Wedding Ring pattern and give it a
twist with un-traditional fabric choices.

Project Note

The dies chosen for this project are only compatible with the AccuQuilt GO!® fabric-cutting system. Refer to the die-cutting general instructions on page 4, for specific die-cutting processes.

Project Specifications

- Skill Level: Advanced
- Size: 86" x 28"

Materials

- 2⅜ yards light floral
- 2¼ yards turquoise dot
- 1½ yards coral graphic print
- ½ yard brown dot
- ½ yard green dot
- Backing 92" x 34"
- Batting 92" x 34"
- Neutral-color all-purpose thread
- 6 (⅞"-diameter) covered buttons
- Washable marker
- AccuQuilt GO! Fabric Cutter
- AccuQuilt GO! Double Wedding Ring, 2-die set (55078)
- Basic sewing supplies and tools

Die-Cutting Instructions

1. Cut four 10" by fabric width strips light floral and fan-fold 10" wide. Die-cut 14 A shapes.

2. Cut three 7½" by fabric width strips light floral and fan-fold 3" wide. Die-cut 37 C shapes.

3. Cut (21) 3½" by fabric width strips turquoise dot fabric and fan-fold 3½" wide. Die-cut 74 E and 74 reverse E (ER) shapes at the same time, and 74 D shapes.

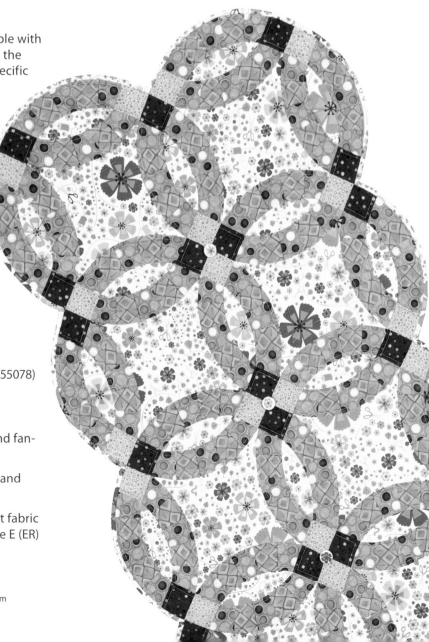

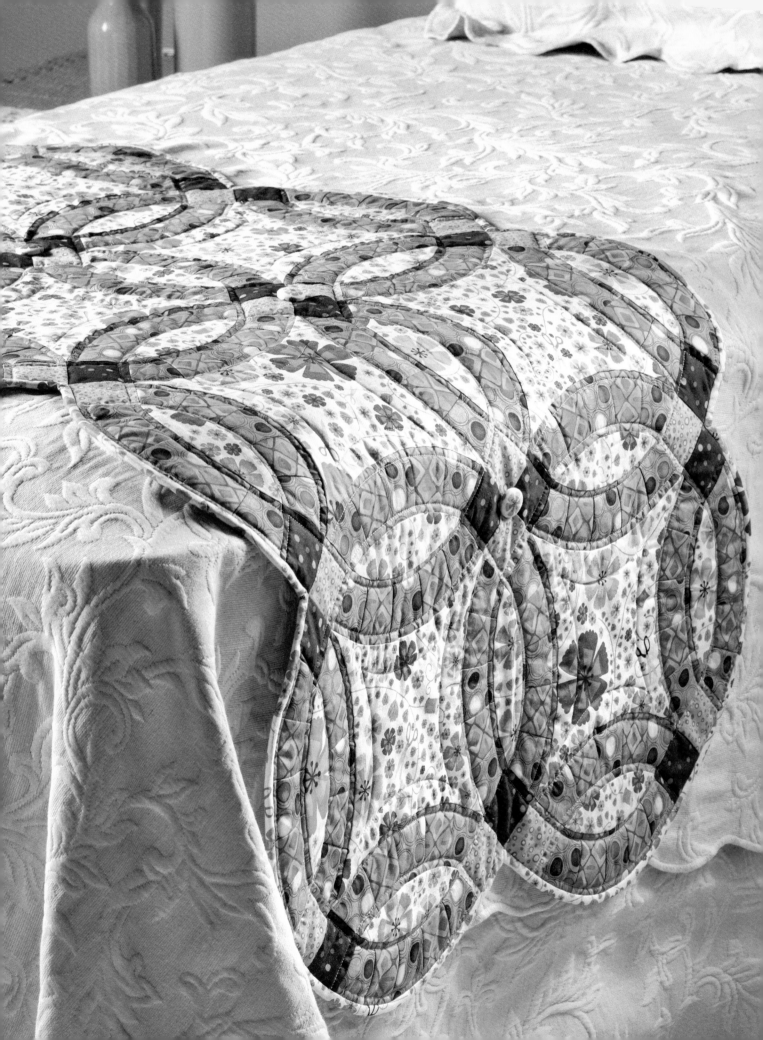

Tip

The B–E shapes are all on one die. When cutting these shapes, place fabric only over shape you wish to cut, using the width strips suggested.

4. Cut (14) 3½" by fabric width strips coral graphic and fan-fold 3½" wide. Die-cut 148 D shapes.

5. Cut four 3½" by fabric width strips each brown dot and green dot, and fan-fold 3½" wide. Die-cut 37 B squares from each fabric.

Additional Cutting Instructions

1. Cut one 18" by fabric width strip light floral; subcut one 18" square. Cut 1¼"-wide bias strips from square; join together to make 245" of single-fold binding.

Completing the Oval Units

1. Stitch one turquoise D, two coral D, and one each turquoise E and ER pieces together referring to Figure 1 for positioning. Press seams in one direction. ***Note:*** *Cut one F from paper. The F piece is a complete arc. Position your pieced fabric arc on top of the F paper arc. If they do not match, adjust seam allowances for a perfect fit.* Repeat to make 74 D/E arc units. Press seams in one direction.

Figure 1

Tip

AccuQuilt GO! Double Wedding Ring die-set shapes A, C, D and E all include joining notches, making piece matching easy, especially on the many curved edges of the Double Wedding Ring pattern.

2. With a washable marker and on the wrong side, mark joining dots ¼" from all four corners of each brown dot and green dot B square and each C point as shown in Figure 2.

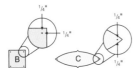

Figure 2

3. Pin and sew a brown B square to one end of a pieced arc, starting and stopping stitching at dots (Figure 3). Press seam toward B square.

Figure 3

4. Pin and sew a green B square to the opposite end of the arc, again starting and stopping stitching at dots (Figure 4). Press seam toward B square.

Figure 4

5. Repeat steps 3 and 4 to make 37 B/D/E arc units

6. Pin and sew a D/E arc unit to C, matching the notches on C and arc center as shown in Figure 5, and starting and stopping stitching at dots marked on C. Press seam toward C.

Figure 5

Tip

To easily sew curved seams, place the convex section on top of the concave section. Pin at the center and both ends, before pinning generously in-between the first three pins. When sewing, remove each pin with the needle in the down position. Handle and press carefully with a dry iron to avoid distortion of the curved shapes' many bias edges.

7. Pin and sew a B/D/E arc unit to the opposite side of C, matching the notches on C and arc center, and starting and stopping stitching at dots marked on B squares (Figure 6). Press seams toward the C shape. Complete the B/E set-in seams. Press seams in same direction as arc seams.

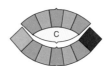

Figure 6

8. Repeat steps 6 and 7 to make a total of 37 oval units.

Completing the Bed Runner Top

1. With a washable marker, mark joining dots ¼" from all four corners on the wrong side of each A shape as shown in Figure 7.

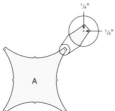

Figure 7

2. Pin and sew an oval unit to A, matching the center notches, and starting and stopping stitching at the dots (Figure 8). Press seam toward A. ***Note:*** *Pay special attention to the positions of the brown and green B squares in the oval units throughout the construction of the Double Wedding Ring rows, referring to the Placement Diagram for color positions.*

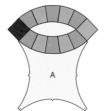

Figure 8

3. Referring to Figure 9, pin and sew a second oval unit to an adjacent side of A, matching the center notches, and starting and stopping stitching at the dots. Press seam toward A. Complete the B/E set-in seams. Press seams in same direction as arc seams.

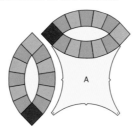

Figure 9

4. Add a third oval unit to the bottom of A as shown in Figure 10, referring to step 3.

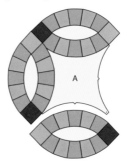

Figure 10

5. Continue adding another A and two oval units to pieced unit from step 4 referring to Figure 11 to complete one vertical X row.

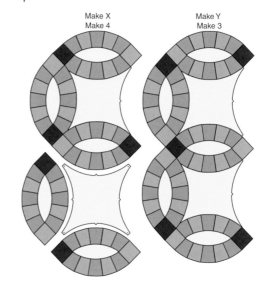

Figure 11

6. Repeat steps 2–5 to make three vertical X rows and four vertical Y rows, again referring to Figure 11 for color placement.

7. Sew the last two oval units to one of the X rows as shown in Figure 12 to make one completed row 7.

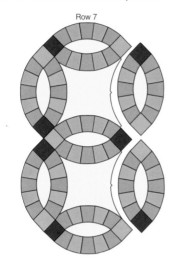

Row 7

Figure 12

8. Arrange and sew the X and Y rows together as shown in Figure 13 to complete the bed runner top.

Row 7

Figure 13

Completing the Quilt

1. Press quilt top on both sides; check for proper seam pressing and trim all loose threads.

2. Sandwich batting between the stitched top and the prepared backing piece; pin or baste layers together to hold. Quilt on marked lines and as desired by hand or machine.

3. When quilting is complete, remove pins or basting. Trim batting and backing fabric edges even with raw edges of quilt top.

4. Baste outer edges together about ³⁄₁₆" from quilt top edge; trim backing and batting even with quilt top.

5. Join binding strips together with diagonal seams; press seams open. Press one short end and one long edge ¼" to wrong side.

6. Starting with the pressed short end and about 4" from an inside point of the curved edges, position the binding raw edge along the quilt raw edges. Use a ¼" seam and stitch binding to quilt until you reach the inside point of the curved edges, stop stitching with the needle down.

7. Lift the presser foot and pivot the quilt and the binding. Using a stiletto or the point of a seam ripper to move any pleats of the binding out of the way, lower the presser foot and take one stitch at a time until the binding evens out, keeping edges even.

8. Continue stitching binding to quilt edges, pivoting at inside points and overlapping the beginning binding end.

9. Turn binding to the back of the quilt and hand-sew in place, covering the stitching line and forming a pleat in the binding at each inside point.

10. Follow manufacturer's instructions and fussy-cut flowers from the remaining light floral to make six covered buttons. Sew one button to the center of each set of four B squares in the center of the bed runner referring to the placement drawing to complete the runner. ❖

Double Wedding Ring Bed Runner
Placement Diagram 86" x 28"

Winding Ways

Design by Connie Kauffman
Quilted by Vickie Hunsberger

Make a gorgeous classic the easy way.

Project Notes

The dies chosen for this project are only compatible with the AccuQuilt GO!® fabric-cutting system. Refer to the die-cutting general instructions on page 4, for specific die-cutting processes.

This quilt was made with 12 light-color fabrics in a variety of golds, tans and reds, and 10 dark-color fabrics in a variety of greens and browns. To make construction figure drawings easier to use, the color key in Figure 1 will be used.

COLOR KEY
- Gold (3 shades)
- Tan (4 shades)
- Red (5 shades)
- Brown (3 shades)
- Green (7 shades)
- Dark Brown (1 shade)

Figure 1

There are two placement diagrams: one shows colors using the color key (Placement Diagram A) and the second shows a closer representation of how the designer used 22 different fabrics in this quilt (Winding Ways). Traditionally, this is a two-color block done in high-contrast lights and darks. This color contrast creates a secondary geometric design of overlapping circles. Since the designer chose a lower-contrast color palette, the overlapping circles are not as evident.

Project Specifications

Skill Level: Advanced
Quilt Size: 46" x 54"
Block Size: 8" x 8"
Number of Blocks: 20

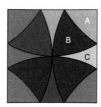

Winding Ways Block
8" x 8"
Make 20

Materials

- 1 fat quarter each, six different red and three different dark brown batiks
- ⅜ yard each three different light gold and four different tan batiks
- ⅝ yard each seven different dark green batiks
- 1⅜ yard brown batik
- Backing 54" x 62"
- Batting 54" x 62"
- Neutral-color all-purpose thread
- Quilting thread
- AccuQuilt GO! Fabric Cutter
- AccuQuilt GO! dies:
    Winding Ways (55069)
    6½" Square (55000)
    3½" Strip Cutter (55032)
- Basic quilting tools and supplies

Die-Cutting Instructions

1. From each light gold and tan batik, cut one 10" by fabric width strip; subcut three 9" x 10" rectangles. Stack 4–6 layers right side up and die-cut 18 light gold and 24 tan each A, B and C pieces using the Winding Ways die.

2. From each red and dark brown batik fat quarters, cut two 9" x 10" rectangles. Stack 4–6 layers right side up and die-cut 24 red and 12 dark brown each A, B and C pieces using the Winding Ways die.

3. Cut one 10" by fabric width strip from each dark green batik; subcut three 9" x 10" rectangles from each strip. Stack 4–6 layers right side up and die-cut 42 each A, B and C pieces using the Winding Ways die. Die-cut four different green batik 6½" G squares from green batik scraps.

4. Cut two 8" by fabric width brown batik strips; fan-fold 8" wide. Die-cut four 3½" strips using the 3½" Strip Cutter. Trim two strips to 3½" x 32½" D strips and two strips to 3½" x 40½" E strips.

Additional Cutting Instructions

1. Cut 2¼" wide brown batik bias strips to make at least a total of 250" bias binding.

2. Cut four 3½" F squares from remainder of brown batik.

Completing Blocks & Half Blocks

1. Referring to Figure 7 for color and orientation, select one A, B and C for Block 1. Liberally pin A to B matching the center notches and ends and carefully stitch the curved seam referring to Figure 2. Clip seam if necessary and press toward B.

Figure 2

2. Add C to A-B, again matching center notches and ends and carefully stitching the curved seam, again referring to Figure 2. Clip seam if necessary and press toward C.

3. Add a second B to the opposite side of C as shown in Figure 3 and a second A to B as shown in Figure 4 in the same manner to make the top half of the Winding Ways block.

Figure 3   **Figure 4**

4. Repeat steps 1–4 to make the bottom half of the Winding Ways block.

5. Add two C pieces to the B edges of the top half of the block as shown in Figure 5.

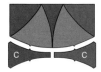

Figure 5

6. Stitch the bottom half of the block to the C edges as shown in Figure 6 to complete Block 1.

Figure 6

7. Repeat steps 1–7 to make a total of 20 Winding Ways blocks referring to Figure 7 for color orientation and number to make. Label each block with the block number used in Figure 7.

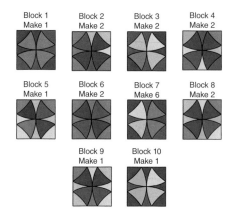

Figure 7

8. Select 36 A, B and C pieces to make 18 Winding Way Half Blocks referring to steps 1–4 and Figure 8. Refer to Placement Diagrams for color orientation.

Winding Way Half Block
Make 18

Figure 8

26

Completing the Quilt

1. Arrange the completed Winding Ways blocks in five rows of four blocks each as shown in Figure 9. *Note: Pay special attention to the orientation of each block. Block orientation makes the interlocking-circle secondary design within the quilt.*

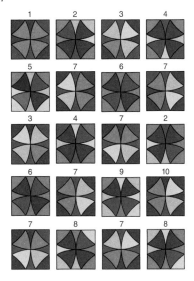

Figure 9

Placement Diagram A

2. Stitch blocks into rows pressing seams in opposite directions between rows and keeping rows in order, again referring to Figure 9.

3. Stitch rows together in numerical order and press seams in one direction.

4. Arrange and stitch four Half Blocks into a top/bottom row referring to Figure 10. Repeat to make two top/bottom rows. Press seams in one direction.

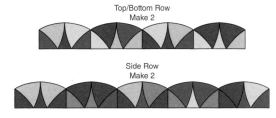

Figure 10

5. Arrange and stitch five Half Blocks into a side row referring again to Figure 10. Press seams in one direction.

6. Draw a diagonal line on the wrong side of each F square. Position an F square in one corner of G as shown in Figure 11 and stitch on the diagonal line. Trim the seam to ¼" and press F away from G. Repeat to make four F-G squares; set aside.

Figure 11

7. Stitch a D strip to the straight edge of each top/bottom Half Block row. Press seam toward D.

8. Stitch D-Half Block rows to the top and bottom of the pieced center referring to Placement Diagram A.

9. Stitch a Half Block side row to E; press seams toward E. Then stitch an F-G square to both ends of the Half Block side row matching the F corner to E. Press seams toward F-G. Repeat to make another side row.

10. Stitch the side rows to opposite sides of the quilt center pressing seams toward E and referring to the Placement Diagram A.

11. Layer and quilt following Finishing Your Quilt on page 6 of General Instructions.

12. Bind the curved quilt edges with bias binding preparing the binding following Finishing Your Quilt on page 6 of General Instructions. Begin applying the binding at the top of a curve, sew to the curve point. Leave the needle in the fabric and raise the presser foot.

Pivot the fabric, folding binding in a small tuck, and continue sewing the binding to the next point. Repeat and complete binding as instructed in Finishing Your Quilt. ❖

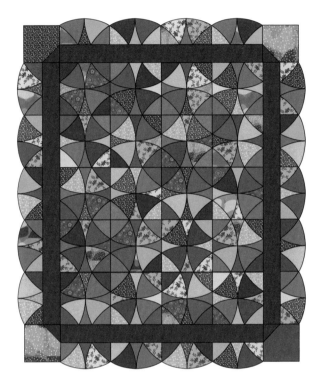

Winding Ways
Placment Diagram 46" x 54"

House of White Birches, Berne, Indiana 46711   Clotilde.com

Fractured Tumblers

Designed & Quilted by Sandra L. Hatch

Put a new twist on an old favorite. Think of all the glorious color combinations you can create.

Project Note

The die chosen for this project is compatible with both the AccuQuilt GO!® and GO! Baby™ fabric-cutting systems. Refer to the die-cutting general instructions on page 4 for specific die-cutting processes.

Project Specifications

Skill Level: Intermediate
Quilt Size: 51½" x 63"

Materials

- 1 fat quarter each cream and brown florals
- ⅞ yard each 7 coordinating fabrics
- 1 yard pink/brown coordinating stripe
- 1 yard green/brown coordinating stripe
- 1⅛ yards gold tonal
- 1⅓ yards dark brown tonal
- Batting 60" x 72"
- Backing 60" x 72"
- Neutral-color all-purpose thread
- Quilting thread
- AccuQuilt GO! Baby Fabric Cutter
- AccuQuilt GO! Tumbler 3½" die (55015)
- Basic quilting tools and supplies

Die-Cutting Instructions

1. Cut two 4½" by fabric width strips from each of the seven coordinating fabrics, and the gold and dark brown tonals; subcut each strip into three 4½" x 12" rectangles.

2. Stack rectangles and die-cut into 162 A tumbler pieces. *Note: There will be extra A pieces to allow you to rearrange pieces to form different patterns.*

3. Cut five 4½" x 12" rectangles from each brown and cream floral fat quarter. Stack rectangles and die-cut the rectangles into 30 A tumbler pieces.

Additional Cutting Instructions

1. Cut four 3½" by fabric width strips from each of the seven coordinating fabrics, and the gold and dark brown tonals for B.

2. Cut nine C strips 1½" by fabric width from each green/brown and pink/brown coordinating stripe.

3. Cut two 1½" x 42" E strips and three 1½" by fabric width D strips gold tonal.

4. Cut one 3½" by fabric width strip gold tonal; subcut four 3½" J squares.

5. Cut five 2½" by fabric width F/G strips pink/brown stripe.

6. Cut six 3½" by fabric width H/I strips dark brown tonal.

7. Cut six 2¼" by fabric width strips green/brown coordinating stripe for binding.

Piecing the B-C-B Tumbler Units

1. Sew a green/brown C strip between two same-fabric B strips to make two B-C-B strip sets from each of the B fabrics to make nine green B-C-B strip sets; press seams away from C.

2. Repeat step 1 with the pink/brown C strips to complete nine pink B-C-B strip sets.

3. Subcut each B-C-B strip set into eight 5" rectangles as shown in Figure 1.

Figure 1

4. Select two B-C-B segments and place on top of the Tumbler die and die-cut a total of 144 B-C-B tumbler units referring to Figure 2.

Figure 2

Completing the Quilt

1. Select 17 A tumbler pieces and B-C-B tumbler units to make a row referring to Figure 3. Repeat to make 17 rows referring to Placement Diagram for positioning of pieces and units. *Note: If forming the pattern shown in the sample quilt, the dark brown tonal and brown floral A pieces form diagonal patterns. The pink A pieces form a pattern down the center with four dark brown tonal B pieces in the center. Pay close attention to the photo and Placement Diagram for positioning of these pieces to from the pattern. If you are not concerned with forming a pattern, you may select the B-C-B units and A pieces randomly.*

Make 17

Figure 3

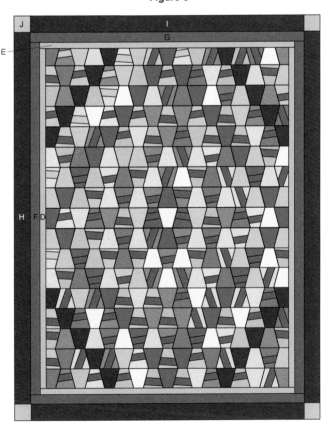

Fractured Tumblers
Placement Diagram 51½" x 63"

2. Select and pin the pieces for just one row at a time, stitching in sets of two as shown in Figure 4; join the sets together in the order as arranged to maintain the established pattern; press seams in adjoining rows in opposite directions.

Figure 4

3. Join the rows as arranged and stitch to complete the pieced center; press seams in one direction.

4. Using a straightedge, trim edges even with the indented ends of the rows as shown in Figure 5. *Note: The trimmed top should measure 40" x 51½" with seams. These are the measurements used to figure the border sizes given here. Adjust sizes as necessary to fit your trimmed center.*

Figure 5

5. Join the D strips on the short ends to make a long strip; press seams open. Subcut strip into two 51½" D strips.

6. Sew the D strips to opposite long sides and E strips to the top and bottom of the pieced center; press seams toward D and E strips.

7. Join the F/G strips on short ends to make one long strip; press seams open. Subcut strip into two 53½" F strips and two 46" G strips.

8. Sew the F strips to opposite long sides and G strips to the top and bottom of the pieced center; press seams toward F and G strips.

9. Join the H/I strips on short ends to make one long strip; press seams open. Subcut strip into two 57½" H strips and two 46" I strips.

10. Sew the H strips to opposite long sides of the pieced center; press seams toward the H strips.

11. Sew a J square to each end of each I strip; press seams toward I strips.

12. Sew an I-J strip to the top and bottom of the pieced center; press seams toward I-J strips.

13. Layer, quilt and bind with 2¼"-wide green/brown coordinating stripe strips, following Finishing Your Quilt on page 6 of the General Instructions. ❖

Circles Squared

Design by Julie Weaver

Even though the Drunkard's Path is a very old quilt block, fabric choices and arranging the blocks in a "layered" design create quite a contemporary look. Add some interest to your decor with this upbeat classic.

Project Note

The die chosen for this project is compatible with both the AccuQuilt GO!® and GO! Baby™ fabric-cutting systems. Refer to the die-cutting general instructions on page 4 for specific die-cutting processes.

Project Specifications

Skill Level: Intermediate
Quilt Size: 40" x 40"
Block Size: 3½" x 3½"
Number of Blocks: 64

Materials

- ¼ yard Fabric 2 (medium brown print)
- ⅓ yard Fabric 3 (tan print), 5 (dark brown print) and 7 (tan print)
- ⅜ yard Fabric 4 (tan print) and 6 (medium brown print)
- ½ yard Fabric 9 (medium brown print)
- ⅝ yard Fabric 8 (dark brown print)
- ⅔ yard Fabric 10 (dark brown solid)
- 1 yard Fabric 1 (brown paisley)
- Neutral-color all-purpose thread
- Quilting thread
- Batting 48" x 48"
- Backing 48" x 48"
- Accuquilt GO! Fabric Cutter
- Accuquilt GO! Drunkard's Path die (55070)
- Basic quilting tools and supplies

Die-Cutting Instructions

1. Cut two 4" by fabric width Fabric 1 strips; subcut (16) 4" squares and label B1.

2. Cut one 5" by fabric width Fabric 2 strip; subcut two 5" x 9" rectangles. Label A2.

> ### Tip
> Because so many fabrics are used to achieve the finished design, special attention must be paid while cutting the fabric and arranging the pieces before sewing. The A and B shapes of the Drunkard's Path block are die-cut separately using nine different fabric colors. Label squares and rectangles as suggested, transferring labels to A and B shapes after die-cutting. Shapes are referred to by these labels in Completing the Blocks.

3. Cut two 4" by fabric width Fabric 3 strips; subcut (12) 4" squares and label B3.

4. Cut two 5" by fabric width Fabric 4 strips; subcut six 5" x 9" rectangles and label A4.

5. Cut two 4" by fabric width Fabric 5 strips; subcut (12) 4" squares and label B5.

6. Cut two 5" by fabric width Fabric 6 strips; subcut six 5" x 9" rectangles and label A6.

7. Cut two 4" by fabric width Fabric 7 strips; subcut (16) 4" squares and label B7.

8. Cut three 5" by fabric width Fabric 8 strips; subcut (12) 5" x 9" rectangles and label A8.

9. Cut two 6" by fabric width Fabric 9 strips; subcut six 6" x 11" rectangles. Die-cut 12 each Fabric 9 A and B pieces. Discard four B pieces. Label A9 and B9.

10. Position B1 pieces, right side up in stacks of 4–6 pieces, on the B areas of the Drunkard's Path die and die-cut 16 B1 shapes. *Note: Refer to block diagrams in Figure 3 for shape of B.*

11. Repeat with all pieces labeled B to die-cut 12 each of B3 and B5 shapes, and 16 B7 shapes.

12. Repeat steps 10 and 11 with all pieces labeled A to die-cut four A2 shapes, 24 A8 shapes and 12 each of A4 and A6 shapes.

Additional Cutting Instructions

1. Cut four 5½" by fabric width Fabric 1 strips; subcut two 30½" E strips and two 40½" F strips for outer borders.

2. Cut four 1½" by fabric width Fabric 10 strips; subcut two 28½" C strips and two 30½" D strips for inner borders.

3. Cut five 2½" by fabric width Fabric 10 strips for binding.

Completing the Blocks

1. Select one each A9 and B1 pieces. With right sides together, match and pin at center notches and ends (Figure 1). Liberally pin curved edges together, gently easing edges to align them referring again to Figure 1.

Figure 1

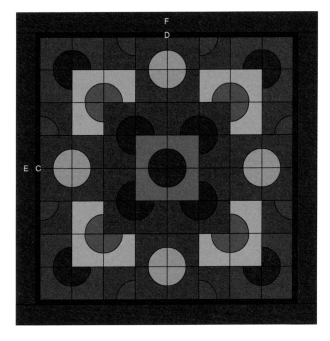

Circles Squared
Placement Diagram 40" x 40"

2. Carefully sew the curved edges together. Clip the concave (edge that curves in) or A9 edge only if necessary; clipping close to but not into the seam line (Figure 2). Carefully press seam toward A9 and flatten using a dry iron.

Figure 2

3. Repeat steps 1 and 2 to make 12 A9/B1 Drunkard's Path blocks. Label this block set as Block 1.

4. Refer to Figure 3 for color and number to construct six different block sets as shown, labeling each set with a block number.

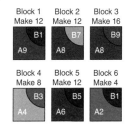

Figure 3

Completing the Quilt

1. Select four Block 1 and two each Block 3 and Block 4. Stitch together as shown in Figure 4 to make Row 1. Press seams in one direction. ***Note:*** *Position and orientation of each block determines the finished design of the quilt. Frequently refer to Figure 4 for correct block placement for the Circles Squared design.* Repeat to make a second Row 1.

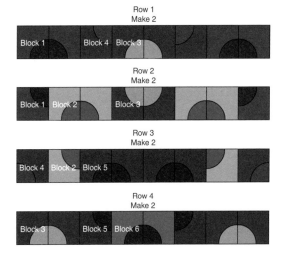

Figure 4

2. Select four Block 2 and two each Block 1 and Block 3. Stitch together, again referring to Figure 4 to make Row 2. Press seams in the opposite direction of Row 1. Repeat to make a second Row 2.

3. Select four Block 5 and two each Block 2 and Block 4. Stitch together, again referring to Figure 4 to make Row 3. Press seams in the opposite direction of Row 2. Repeat to make a second Row 3.

4. Select four Block 3 and two each Block 5 and Block 6. Stitch together, again referring to Figure 4 to make Row 4. Press seams in the opposite direction of Row 3. Repeat to make a second Row 4.

5. Arrange and stitch rows together Rows 1–4 and then Rows 4–1 as shown in Figure 5. Press seams in one direction to complete quilt center.

Figure 5

6. Sew C strips to opposite sides of quilt center and D strips to remaining opposite sides. Press seams toward C and D.

7. Sew E borders to C sides of quilt center; press seams toward E. Sew F borders to remaining sides of quilt center; press seams toward F.

8. Layer, quilt and bind using Fabric 10 2½" binding strips following Finishing Your Quilt on page 6 of General Instructions. ❖

Dancing Pinwheels

Designed & Quilted by Sandy Boobar &
Sue Harvey of Pine Tree Country Quilts

This quilt is much easier than it looks. The dancing pinwheels
will delight you when you see just how easy they can be.

Project Note

The die chosen for this project is compatible with
both the AccuQuilt GO!® and GO! Baby™ fabric-cutting
systems. Refer to the die-cutting general instructions on
page 4, for specific die-cutting processes.

Project Specifications

- Skill Level: Intermediate
- Quilt Size: 44½" x 53"
- Block Size: 8" x 8"
- Number of Blocks: 20

Dancing Pinwheel
8" x 8" Block
Make 20

Materials

- 1⅛ yard lavender tonal
- 1⅞ yards pink tonal
- 2½ yards dragonfly print
- Batting 53" x 61"
- Backing 53" x 61"
- Neutral-color all-purpose thread
- Coordinating pink quilting thread
- AccuQuilt GO! Baby Fabric Cutter
- AccuQuilt GO! Apple Core die C (55036)
- 8½" x 8½" square ruler
- Basic quilting tools and supplies

Die-Cutting Instructions

1. Cut seven 8" by fabric width strips dragonfly print
and fan-fold 6½" wide. Die-cut 40 C shapes. **Note:** If you
cannot cut six layers of your fabric choice, subcut strips into
(40) 6½" x 8" C rectangles. Layer C rectangles and die-cut.
Repeat to die-cut 40 C shapes.

Additional Cutting Instructions

1. Cut (10) 3½" by fabric width B strips lavender tonal.

2. Cut (10) 3½" by fabric width A strips pink tonal.

3. Cut eight 1" by fabric width strips pink tonal. Subcut
strips into four 1" x 34" E strips and (15) 1" x 8½" D strips.

4. Cut four 1½" by fabric width F/G strips pink tonal

5. Cut five 2½" by fabric width J/K strips pink tonal.

6. Cut five 3" by fabric width H/I strips dragonfly print.

7. Cut five 2¼" by fabric width strips dragonfly print
for binding.

Constructing A-B Four-Patch Units

1. Sew an A strip to a B strip along the length to make
an A/B strip set; press seam toward A. Repeat to make a
total of 10 A/B strip sets.

2. Subcut the A/B strip sets into (80) 5" A/B segments as
shown in Figure 1.

Figure 1

3. Join two A/B segments to make an A/B Four-Patch unit as shown in Figure 2; press seam in one direction. Repeat to make a total of 40 A/B Four-Patch units.

Make 40

Figure 2

4. Layer four A/B Four-Patch units right side up on the GO! Apple Core die, covering the outline of the shape and die-cut.

5. Repeat, positioning the A/B Four-Patch units on the die in different orientations for variety in the A/B apple-core shapes, and die-cut a total of 40 A/B apple-core units. ***Note:*** *To have even more variety in the A/B apple-core units, cut them individually instead of in sets of 4.*

Completing the Blocks

1. Position and pin a C shape right sides together with an A/B shape as shown in Figure 3; matching the center notches and the outside corners.

Figure 3

2. Sew the pieces together to make a section as shown in Figure 4; press the seam toward the A-B shape.

Figure 4

3. Repeat steps 1 and 2 to make a second section.

4. Position and pin the sections right sides together, matching the center notches, outside corners and seam. ***Note:*** *Be careful not to pull the seams apart or stretch the curves.*

5. Sew the sections together to make a block unit as shown in Figure 5; press the seam toward the C shapes.

Figure 5

6. Repeat steps 1–5 to make a total of 20 block units.

7. Center the square ruler on the intersection of the A/B and C shapes in the block unit and trim each block unit to 8½" x 8½" to complete 20 Dancing Pinwheel blocks as shown in Figure 6.

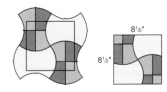

8½"

8½"

Figure 6

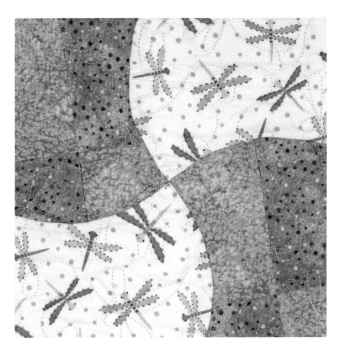

Completing the Quilt

1. Join four blocks with three D strips to make a row as shown in Figure 7; press seams toward D. Turn every other block to position C pieces across from each other. Repeat to make a total of five rows.

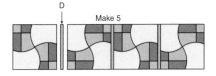

D

Make 5

Figure 7

2. Arrange rows with E strips referring to Figure 8, turning every other row to form a secondary design at the block intersections. Press seams toward E strips.

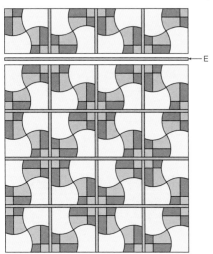

Figure 8

3. Join the F/G strips on the short ends to make a long strip; press seams to one side. Cut two 42½" F strips and two 36" G strips.

4. Sew the F strips to opposite long sides and the G strips to the top and bottom of the pieced center; press seams toward the strips.

5. Join the H/I strips on the short ends to make a long strip; press seams to one side. Cut two 44½" H strips and two 41" I strips.

6. Sew the H strips to opposite long sides and the I strips to the top and bottom of the pieced center; press seams toward the strips.

7. Join the J/K strips on the short ends to make a long strip; press seams to one side. Cut two 49½" J strips and two 45" K strips.

8. Sew the J strips to opposite long sides and the K strips to the top and bottom of the pieced center to complete the top; press seams toward the strips.

9. Layer, quilt and bind referring to Finishing Your Quilt on page 6 of General Instructions. ❖

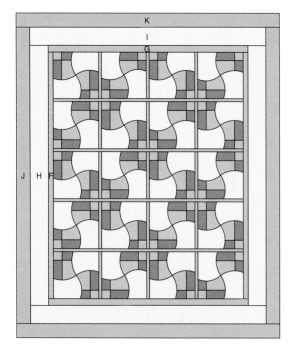

Dancing Pinwheels
Placement Diagram 44½" x 53"

Baby Bubbles

Design by Gina Gempesaw
Quilted by Carole Whaling

Take this to the next baby shower.

Project Note
The dies chosen for this project are only compatible with the AccuQuilt GO!® fabric-cutting system. Refer to the die-cutting general instructions on page 4 for specific die-cutting processes.

Project Specifications
Skill Level: Confident Beginner
Quilt Size: 46" x 53"
Block Size: 7" x 7"
Number of Blocks: 21

Baby Bubbles
7" x 7" Block
Make 21

Materials
- 11 fat quarters assorted coordinating blue and green prints
- ¾ yard blue/green plaid
- 2 yards coordinating light background print
- Backing 54" x 61"
- Batting 54" x 61"
- Neutral-color all-purpose thread
- Quilting thread to match
- AccuQuilt GO! Fabric Cutter
- AccuQuilt GO! dies:
    Rob Peter to Pay Paul, 2-die set (55068)
    2½" Strip Cutter (55017)
    2¼" Strip Cutter (55053)
- Basic quilting tools and supplies

Die-Cutting Instructions
1. From each fat quarter, cut one 7½" x 18" rectangle; subcut two 7½" squares to make 22 C squares; discard one.

2. From each fat quarter, cut two 6" x 18" rectangles; subcut four 6" x 9" rectangles. Die-cut eight Rob Peter to Pay Paul B edges as shown in Figure 1 below from each fabric, totaling 168.

3. Cut six 9" by fabric width light background print strips; fan-fold 9" wide. Die-cut 21 Rob Peter to Pay Paul for A centers again referring to Figure 1 below.

4. Cut three 6" by fabric width light background print strips; fan-fold 6" wide. Using 2½" strip cutter die-cut six D-E strips.

5. Cut one 10" by fabric width strip and one 6" by fabric width strip from blue/green plaid; fan-fold strips 10" wide. Using 2¼" strip cutter die-cut six 2¼" strips for binding.

Completing Blocks & Rows
1. Arrange A, B and C pieces in seven rows referring to Figure 1, matching B edges to C squares and adding extra B edges to A pieces on the outside edges of rows. *Note: B and C pieces will form circles throughout the quilt pieced center.*

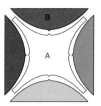

Figure 1

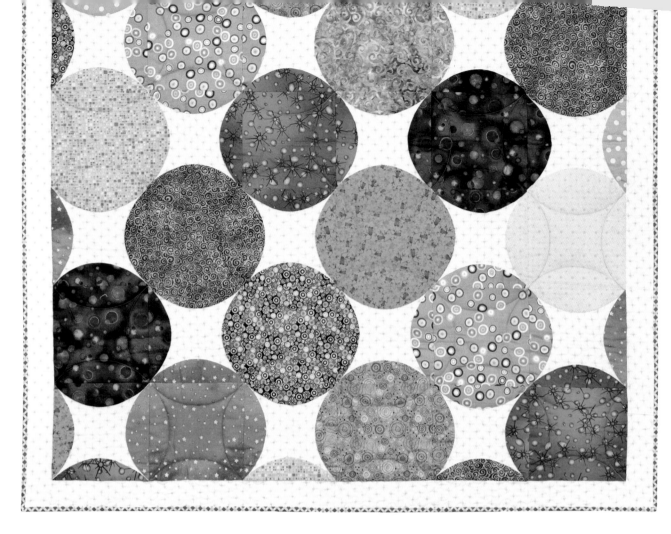

2. To complete one Rob Peter to Pay Paul block, select first A and corresponding B edges from row 1. With B on top of A, pin at center notches, curve ends and generously pin between notches referring to Figure 2. Carefully stitch curved seam and press toward B. Repeat to stitch all B edges to A to complete one block. Return completed block to arrangement and repeat to make 21 blocks.

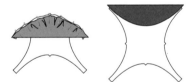

Figure 2

3. Join pieced Rob Peter to Pay Paul blocks to C squares as arranged referring again to Figure 1 to make seven rows, pressing seams in opposite directions.

4. Join rows, matching seams, in order referring to Figure 1. Press seams in one direction.

Completing the Quilt

1. Join D-E strips on short ends to make one long strip, press seams to one side. Cut two 42½" D borders and two 53½" E borders.

2. Stitch D to top and bottom of quilt center and E to opposite sides. Press seams toward D and E.

3. Layer, quilt and bind with blue/green plaid 2¼" strips following Finishing Your Quilt on page 6 in General Instructions. ❖

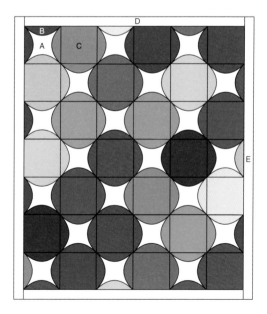

Baby Bubbles
Placement Diagram 46" x 53"

Roundabout

Design by Gina Gempesaw
Quilted by Carol Whaling

Believe it or not, this quilt was made with seven
AccuQuilt dies. Only the wide borders were rotary-cut.
Obviously, the options are endless with AccuQuilt.

Project Note

All of the dies chosen for this project are compatible
with the AccuQuilt GO!®, only some are compatible
with the GO! Baby™. Check the GO! Die & Cutter
Compatibility Chart for the dies that are compatible with
the GO! Baby. Refer to the die-cutting general instructions on page 4 for specific die-cutting processes.

Project Specifications

Skill Level: Beginner
Quilt Size: 84" x 84"
Block Size: 18" x 18"
Number of Blocks: 9

Materials

- ⅝ yard large flower print
- 2 yards turquoise dots
- 2⅛ yards cream tonal
- 2⅛ yards green plaid
- 2⅛ yards orange
- 2½ yards blue print
- 2½ yards red tonal
- Backing 92" x 92"
- Batting 92" x 92"
- Neutral-color all-purpose thread
- Quilting thread
- AccuQuilt GO! Fabric Cutter
- AccuQuilt GO! dies:
    6½" Square A (55000)
    3½" Strip Cutter (55032)
    √Chisels C (55039)
    Drunkard's Path—3½" finished F & G (55070)
    √Half Square—3" finished triangle E (55009)
    √3½" x 6½" Rectangle H (55005)
    √3½" Square B (55006)
- Basic quilting tools and supplies

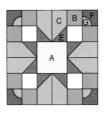

Roundabout Block
18" x 18"
Make 9

Die-Cutting Instructions

1. Cut two 7½" by fabric width large flower print strips and fan-fold 7½" wide. Die-cut 10 A shapes; discard one.

2. Cut six 8" by fabric width cream tonal strips and fan-fold five strips 4½" wide. Die-cut 80 B squares.

3. Cut one 4½" by fabric width cream tonal strip and individually die-cut four B squares for a total of 84 cream tonal B squares.

4. Cut three 7½" by fabric width cream tonal strips and fan-fold 4½" wide. Die-cut 24 H rectangles.

5. Cut eight 8" by fabric width green plaid strips and fan-fold 4½" wide. Die-cut 128 B squares; discard eight squares.

6. Cut three 11" by fabric width strips each turquoise dot and orange. Layer a turquoise dot and orange strip right sides together and fan-fold 4½". Die-cut 16 C chisel shapes. Repeat with remaining strips to die-cut a total of 36 turquoise dot and orange C sets.

7. Cut three 3½" by fabric width turquoise dot strips and fan-fold 3½" wide. Die-cut 36 G Drunkard's Path pieces.

8. Cut one 24" by fabric width strip and one 8" by fabric width strip from remaining orange. Fan-fold strips 8" wide and use Strip Cutter to die-cut a total of eight strips for D/I borders.

9. Cut one 8" by fabric width red tonal strip and fan-fold 4½" wide. Die-cut 16 B squares.

10. Cut three 9½" by fabric width red tonal strips and fan-fold 4½" wide. Die-cut a total of 72 E triangles.

11. Cut four 4½" by fabric width red tonal and fan-fold 4½" wide. Die-cut 36 F Drunkard's Path pieces.

Additional Cutting Instructions

1. Cut nine 2¼" by fabric width red tonal for binding.

2. Cutting along fabric length, cut two 6½" x 72½" J border strips and two 6½" x 84½" K border strips from the blue print fabric.

Completing Roundabout Block

1. Match and pin center notches and ends of F and G right sides together with G on top as shown in Figure 1.

Figure 1

2. Stitch to first pin, lower needle, remove pin and pivot fabric until lying flat. Then stitch to next pin and repeat. Continue stitching in this manner to complete the curved seam (Figure 2).

Figure 2

3. Clip seam allowance and press toward F to complete one Drunkard's Path unit, again referring to Figure 2.

4. Repeat steps 1–3 to make 36 Drunkard's Path units.

5. Sew one Drunkard's Path unit to a green plaid B as shown in Figure 3 to make a G/F/B row. Press seam toward B. Sew a green plaid B and cream tonal B together to make a B/B row, again referring to Figure 3. Press seam toward green plaid B.

Figure 3

6. Sew rows together to make a Four-Patch unit, again referring to Figure 3. Press seam toward G/F/B row.

7. Repeat steps 5 and 6 to make 36 Four-Patch units.

8. Sew an E triangle to a turquoise dot C as shown in Figure 4. Press seam toward C. Repeat to make 36 turquoise dot chisel rectangles.

9. Repeat step 7 with an E triangle and an orange C to make 36 orange chisel rectangles, again referring to Figure 4.

Figure 4

10. Sew a turquoise dot and orange chisel rectangle right sides together matching the C sides (Figure 5). Press seam toward turquoise dot chisel rectangle.

Figure 5

11. Repeat step 10 to make 36 chisel units.

12. Referring to Figure 6 for unit positioning, sew a chisel unit between two Four–Patch units to make a top row; sew A between two chisel units to make a center row

and sew another chisel unit between two Four–Patch units to make a bottom row. Press seams in direction of arrows shown in Figure 6.

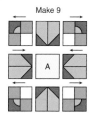

Make 9

Figure 6

13. Repeat to make nine Roundabout Blocks.

Completing Sashing Strips & Rows

1. To make a sashing strip, sew two each cream tonal and green plaid B squares and one H rectangle together as shown in Figure 7. Press seams toward green plaid B squares.

Make 24

Figure 7

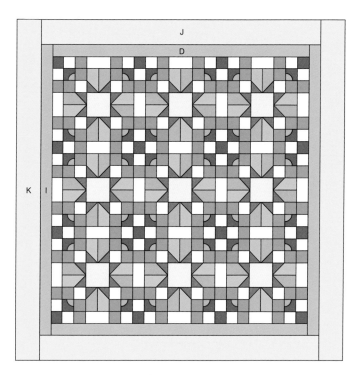

Roundabout
Placement Diagram 84" x 84"

2. Repeat to make 24 sashing strips. Set aside 12 sashing strips to make block rows.

3. To make a sashing row, sew three sashing strips and four red tonal B squares together alternately beginning and ending with B squares (Figure 8). Press seams toward red tonal B squares. Repeat to make four sashing rows.

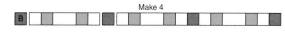

Make 4

Figure 8

Completing the Quilt

1. Sew three Roundabout blocks and four sashing strips together alternately beginning and ending with a sashing strip (Figure 9). Repeat to make three block rows.

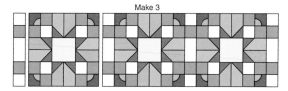

Make 3

Figure 9

2. Sew three block rows and four sashing rows together alternately beginning and ending with a sashing row referring to the Placement Diagram for positioning.

3. Sew the D/I border strips together on short ends and press seams open. Cut two 66½" D borders and two 72½" I borders.

4. Sew D to top and bottom of pieced center and I to both sides referring to the placement diagram. Press seams toward D and I.

5. Sew J to the top and bottom, and K to opposite sides of the quilt top. Press seams toward J and K.

6. Layer, quilt and bind referring to Finishing Your Quilt on page 6 of General Instructions. ❖

48

Scrappy Braid

Designed & Quilted by Sandra L. Hatch

Got scraps? Well here is the perfect solution to piles of beautiful leftover fabric—the more variety, the better for this project.

Project Note

The die chosen for this project is compatible with both the AccuQuilt GO!® and GO! Baby™ fabric cutting systems. Refer to the die-cutting general instructions on page 4 for specific die-cutting processes.

Project Specifications

Skill Level: Intermediate
Quilt Size: 62" x 77¾"

Materials

- 8 (4" x 11") scrap rectangles each in the following colors: white/red, dark red, light and dark green, light and dark blue, light and dark brown, light and dark orange, yellow, light and dark purple, light pink and raspberry
- ⅞ yard green tonal
- 2 yards black multicolored circle print
- Batting 70" x 86"
- Backing 70" x 86"
- Neutral-color all-purpose thread
- Quilting thread
- AccuQuilt GO! Baby Fabric Cutter
- AccuQuilt GO! Chisels die A (55039)
- Basic quilting tools and supplies

Tip

If you would like the freedom to audition different fabrics, cut extra A and AR pieces from each color. It's so easy to cut the pieces with the AccuQuilt GO! Baby that you could cut enough for two quilts at one time.

Die-Cutting Instructions

1. Stack three or four layers of the 4" x 11" scrap rectangles right sides together to cut A and reverse A pieces (AR) at the same time. Die-cut a total of 16 each of each color to total 120 A pieces and 120 AR pieces using the Chisels die. Select one color and cut eight each extra A and AR pieces to fill in ends.

Additional Cutting Instructions

1. Cut six 1½" by fabric width B/C strips green tonal.

2. Cut seven 2¼" by fabric width strips green tonal for binding.

3. Cut four 6½" x 72" D/E strips along the length of the black multicolored circles print.

Completing a Braid Row

1. Decide on the color order in which you want the rows to appear. In the sample quilt the order starts at the bottom with the white/red and moves to dark red, light green, dark green, light blue, dark blue, light brown, dark brown, light orange, dark orange, yellow, light purple, dark purple, light pink and raspberry.

2. Select and arrange the A and AR pieces for one row referring to Figure 1.

3. Select the first A and AR pieces at the bottom of the row and place piece 1 right sides together with piece 2 as shown in Figure 2; starting at the top edge, sew to within ¾" of the end of the seam, again referring to Figure 2. Open and press the seam toward piece 1.

Figure 1

Figure 2

4. Add piece 3 to the pieced unit as shown in Figure 3; press seam toward piece A3.

Figure 3

5. Continue adding pieces in the same manner until the row is complete as shown in Figure 4. *Note: The sample has 15 pieces on the left edge of each row at this time; refer to the Placement Diagram.*

Figure 4

6. Repeat Steps 1–5 to complete a total of eight braid rows. *Note: The sample shown has three reversed rows, which makes the design zigzag in an interesting pattern across the quilt. If you want a symmetrical quilt, make four braid rows and four reversed braid rows referring to Figure 5.*

Row   Reversed Row

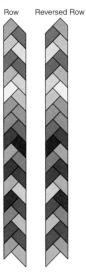

Figure 5

7. Arrange and join the rows, matching same-color fabric edges as shown in Figure 6; press seams in one direction. *Note: If using an equal number of reversed strips, alternate strips to create a pattern.*

Reversed Rows

Figure 6

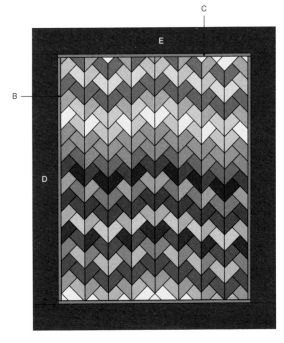

Scrappy Braid
Placement Diagram 62" x 77³/₄"

8. Decide where you want the top and bottom to be trimmed and select the fill-in A and AR pieces. Sew these pieces in place and complete the partial seams.

9. Select the lowest point on the top and bottom edges, and using a straight edge, trim even with this edge across the top as shown in Figure 7 to complete the pieced center.

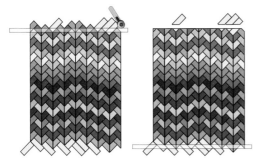

Figure 7

Completing the Quilt

1. Measure the quilt top through the center vertically and horizontally and record measurements. Repeat for outer side, top and bottom edges—the measurements should be the same as the center. If they are not, use the center measurements to cut border sizes. **Note:** *The measurements given here refer to the sample quilt as shown.*

2. Join the B/C strips on short ends to make one long strip; press seams open. Subcut strip into two 50½" C strips and two 64¼" B strips.

3. Sew B strips to opposite sides and C strips to the top and bottom of the pieced center; press seams toward B and C strips.

4. Subcut D/E strips into two 66¼" D strips and two 62½" E strips.

5. Sew D strips to opposite sides and E strips to the top and bottom of the pieced center; press seams toward B and C strips.

6. Layer, quilt and bind with 2¼"-wide green tonal strips, following Finishing Your Quilt on page 6 of the General Instructions. ❖

House of White Birches, Berne, Indiana 46711   Clotilde.com

Snails' Trail

Designed & Quilted by Julia Dunn

Take a traditional block pattern and make it fresh
and modern with your color choices.

Project Note

All of the dies chosen for this project are compatible with both the AccuQuilt GO!® and AccuQuilt GO! Baby™ fabric-cutting systems. Refer to AccuQuilt GO! die-cutting general instructions on page 4 for specific die-cutting processes.

Project Specifications

Skill Level: Confident Beginner
Quilt Size: 62" x 62"
Block Size: 7" x 7"
Number of Blocks: 64

Snails' Trail
7" x 7" Block
Make 64

Materials

- 32 fat eighths variety red prints
- 32 fat eighths variety black-and-white prints
- 1¼ yard solid black
- Backing 70" x 70"
- Batting 70" x 70"
- Neutral-color all-purpose thread
- Quilting thread
- 64 sheets 8½" x 11" tissue paper
- AccuQuilt GO! Baby Fabric Cutter
- AccuQuilt GO! dies:
    - Value Die (55018)
    - Half Square—3" Finished Triangle (55009)
    - Half Square—4" Finished Triangle (55031)
- Basic quilting tools and supplies

Die-Cutting Instructions

1. From each red print fat eighth, cut one 5½" x 22" strip; subcut one each 5½" x 11½" strip and 5½" x 9½" strip. From each red print fat eighth, cut two 3" x 4" strips and two 2" x 4" A strips. Keep all same-color strips together in sets.

2. From each black-and-white print fat eighth, cut one 5½" x 22" strip; subcut one each 5½" x 11½" strip and 5½" x 9½" strip. From each black-and-white print fat eighth, cut two 3" x 4" strips and two 2" x 4" B strips. Keep all same-color strips together in sets.

3. Select a red strip set and a black-and-white strip set. Stack same-size strips right sides up to cut pieces for two blocks using the same red and black-and-white color combination.

4. Die-cut two sets of 4" triangles from the 5½" x 11½" red and black-and-white strip set.

5. Die-cut two sets of 3" finished triangles from the 5½" x 9½" red and black-and-white strip set.

6. Die-cut two sets of 2" triangles from the 3" x 4" red and black-and-white strip set.

7. Repeat steps 3–6 to cut pieces for 64 blocks. Sort pieces into block sets that include two each of 2", 3" and 4" triangles in red and black-and-white, and one each A strip and B strip; all from the same red and black-and-white strip sets.

Additional Cutting Instructions

1. Cut six 3½" by fabric width solid black C/D strips.

2. Cut seven 2¼" by fabric width strips from solid black for binding. ***Note:*** *The 2¼" Strip Cutter die (55053) can be used to cut these strips if you are using an AccuQuilt GO! Fabric Cutter. It is not compatible with the GO! Baby. Refer to the GO! Fabric Reference Chart at www.accuquilt.com for yardage needed.*

Completing the Blocks

1. Trace foundation piecing pattern onto tissue paper, transferring all numbers and lines to make a paper-piecing pattern. Repeat to make 64 foundation paper-piecing patterns. *Note: Save time by using a copier to make 64 copies on standard copy paper.*

2. Set machine stitch length to a short setting, at least 18–20 stitches per inch.

3. To complete one block, select a block set. Stitch A and B strips along length right sides together; press seam toward B. Cut the A-B strip set into two 2" A-B units (Figure 1).

Figure 1

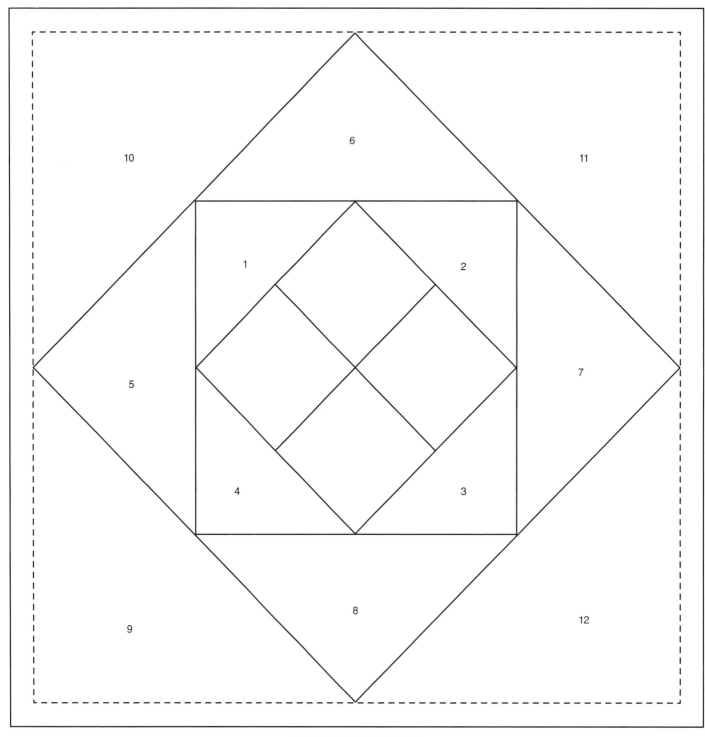

Foundation Piecing Pattern

4. Stitch the A-B units together to make a Four-Patch unit as shown in Figure 2. Press seam to one side.

Figure 2

5. With the right side of paper pattern facing down, pin the Four-Patch unit, right side up, to the wrong side of the paper centered over the Four-Patch center area on pattern. Place a red 2" triangle right sides together on the Four-Patch unit ¼" past the shared line between the center Four-Patch area and area 1 as shown in Figure 3 and pin in place.

Figure 3

6. Flip paper over and stitch along the Four-Patch area and area 1 shared line. Turn paper over and press the 2" triangle away from the Four-Patch unit (Figure 4).

Figure 4

7. Position and stitch a black 2" triangle along the shared line of the Four-Patch center area and area 2 (Figure 5). Press the black 2" triangle away from the Four Patch unit (Figure 6).

Figure 5

Figure 6

8. Stitch the remaining pieces in numerical order using black 2", 3" and 4" triangles in areas 2, 4, 6, 8, 11 and 9, and using red 2", 3" and 4" triangles in areas 1, 3, 5, 7, 10 and 12.

9. Trim the completed pieced block along solid outer line of paper pattern. Do not remove paper at this time.

10. Repeat steps 3–9 to make 64 foundation-pieced Snails' Trail blocks.

Continued on page 63

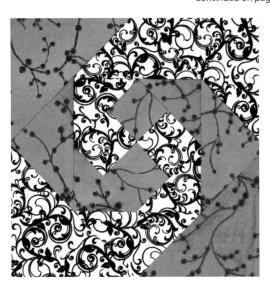

Snails' Trail
Placement Diagram 62" x 62"

House of White Birches, Berne, Indiana 46711   Clotilde.com

Tied With a Bow

Design by Sue Harvey & Sandy Boobar of Pine Tree Country Quilts

Make a special gift quilt.

Project Note

All of the dies chosen for this project are compatible with both the AccuQuilt GO!® and AccuQuilt GO! Baby™ fabric-cutting systems. Refer to AccuQuilt GO! die-cutting general instructions on page 3, for specific die-cutting processes.

Project Specifications

Skill Level: Confident Beginner
Quilt Size: 75" x 89"
Block Size: 14" x 14"
Number of Blocks: 20

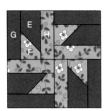

Dark Bow
14" x 14" Block
Make 10

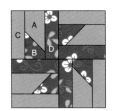

Light Bow
14" x 14" Block
Make 10

Materials

- 1⅝ yards light blue floral
- 2½ yards tan tonal
- 2⅓ yards dark blue tonal
- 2¾ yards medium blue floral
- Batting 83" x 97"
- Backing 83" x 97"
- Neutral-color all-purpose thread
- Coordinating tan quilting thread
- AccuQuilt GO! Baby Fabric Cutter
- AccuQuilt GO! dies:
  ✓ Chisels (55039)
  ✓ 2½" Strip Cutter (55014)
- Basic sewing tools and supplies

Die-Cutting Instructions

1. Cut two 11" by fabric width strips light blue floral; subcut into (18) 4½" x 11" rectangles. Cut one 4½" by fabric width strip light blue floral; subcut into two 4½" x 11" rectangles to make a total of 20 rectangles. Stack rectangles right side up in four stacks of five pieces. Die-cut 40 F Chisel shapes.

2. Cut four 6" by fabric width light blue floral strips; fan-fold 6" wide. Using strip cutter, die-cut eight 2½" H strips.

3. Cut two 11" by fabric width strips tan tonal; subcut into (18) 4½" x 11" rectangles. Cut one 4½" by fabric width strip tan tonal; subcut into two 4½" x 11" rectangles to make a total of 20 rectangles. Stack rectangles right side up in four stacks of five pieces. Die-cut 40 A Chisel shapes.

4. Cut four 6" by fabric width tan tonal strips; fan-fold 6" wide. Using strip cutter, die-cut eight 2½" C strips.

5. Cut four 6" by fabric width tan tonal strips; fan-fold 6" wide. Using strip cutter, die-cut seven 2½" by fabric width K/L strips.

6. Cut two 11" by fabric width strips dark blue tonal; subcut into (18) 4½" x 11" rectangles. Cut one 4½" by fabric width strip dark blue tonal; subcut into two 4½" x 11" rectangles to make a total of 20 rectangles. Stack rectangles right side up in four stacks of five pieces. Die-cut 40 E Chisel shapes.

7. Cut four 6" by fabric width dark blue tonal strips; fan-fold 6" wide. Using strip cutter, die-cut eight 2½" by fabric width G strips.

8. Cut two 11" by fabric width strips medium blue floral; subcut into (18) 4½" x 11" rectangles. Cut one 4½" by fabric width strip medium blue floral; subcut into two 4½" x 11" rectangles to make a total of 20 rectangles. Stack rectangles right side up in four stacks of five pieces. Die-cut 40 B Chisel shapes.

9. Cut four 6" by fabric width medium blue floral strips; fan-fold 6" wide. Using strip cutter, die-cut eight 2½" by fabric width D strips.

Additional Cutting Instructions

1. Cut the eight 2½" light blue floral H strips into (40) 2½" x 7½" H rectangles.

2. Cut four 2" J squares from tan tonal.

3. Cut the eight 2½" tan tonal C strips into (40) 2½" x 7½" C rectangles.

4. Cut seven 1½" by fabric width M/N strips tan tonal. *Note: The 1½" Strip Cutter die (55024) can be used to cut these strips if you are using an AccuQuilt GO! Fabric Cutter. It is not compatible with the GO! Baby. Refer to the GO! Fabric Reference Chart at www.accuquilt.com for yardage needed.*

5. Cut the eight 2½" dark blue tonal G strips into (40) 2½" x 7½" G rectangles.

6. Cut four 2" by fabric width strips dark blue tonal; subcut into (45) 2" x 3½" I pieces.

7. Cut nine 2¼" by fabric width strips dark blue tonal for binding. *Note: The 2¼" Strip Cutter die (55053) can be used to cut these strips if you are using an AccuQuilt GO! Fabric Cutter. It is not compatible with the GO! Baby. Refer to the GO! Fabric Reference Chart at www.accuquilt.com for yardage needed.*

8. Cut the eight 2½" medium blue floral D strips into (40) 2½" x 7½" D rectangles.

9. Cut eight 5½" by fabric width O/P strips medium blue floral.

Completing the Bow Blocks

1. Sew an A piece to a B piece as shown in Figure 1; press seam toward the B piece. Repeat to make 40 A-B units.

Make 40

Figure 1

2. Repeat step 1 with E and F pieces to make 40 E-F units as shown in Figure 2; press seams toward the E pieces.

Make 40

Figure 2

3. Trim 2" from the B end of each A-B unit as shown in Figure 3; label the trimmed-off pieces BB. Repeat to trim 2" from the F end of each E-F unit; label the trimmed-off pieces FF. Set the BB and FF pieces aside for the pieced border.

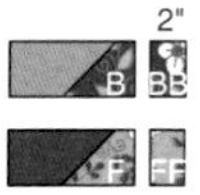

Figure 3

4. Sew an A-B unit between a C and D piece to make a light quarter unit as shown in Figure 4; press seams toward the D and C pieces. Repeat to make 40 light quarter units.

Make 40   Make 40

Figure 4

5. Repeat step 4 with the E-F units and G and H pieces to make 40 dark quarter units, again referring to Figure 4.

6. To complete one Light Block, join two light quarter units to make a row as shown in Figure 5; press seam toward the D edge. Repeat to make a second row. Join the rows to complete one Light Block; press seam in one direction. Repeat to make 10 blocks.

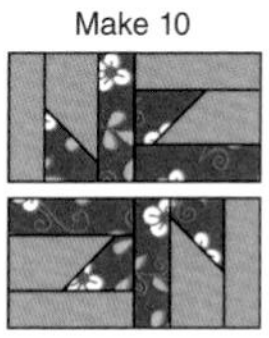

Make 10

Figure 5

7. Repeat step 6 with the dark quarter units to complete 10 Dark Blocks as shown in Figure 6.

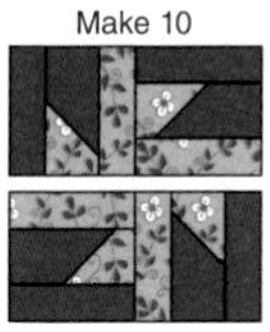

Make 10

Figure 6

Completing the Quilt

1. Join two Light Blocks with two Dark Blocks to make a block row as shown in Figure 7; press seams toward the Dark Blocks. Repeat to make a total of five block rows.

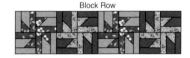

Block Row

Figure 7

2. Join the block rows to complete the pieced center, turning every other row to alternate Light and Dark Blocks from row to row referring to Placement Diagram for positioning; press seams in one direction.

3. Join the K/L strips on the short ends to make a long strip; press seams to one side. Subcut into two 70½" K strips and two 60½" L strips.

4. Sew the K strips to opposite long sides and the L strips to the top and bottom of the pieced center; press seams toward the strips.

5. Select and join 13 I pieces with six each FF and BB pieces to make the left border strip as shown in Figure 8; press seams toward the I pieces. Trim the strip to 74½". Sew the strip to the left side of the pieced center; press seam toward the strip.

Top/Bottom Border
Make 2

Left Side Border
Make 1

Right Side Border
Make 1

Figure 8

6. Select and join 12 I pieces with seven FF pieces and six BB pieces to make the right border strip, again referring to Figure 8; press seams toward the I pieces. Trim the strip to 74½". Sew the strip to the right side of the pieced center; press seam toward the strip.

7. Select and join 10 I pieces with five each FF and BB pieces and two J squares to make the top border strip, again referring to Figure 8; press seams toward the I pieces. Repeat to make the bottom border strip. Sew the strips to the top and bottom of the quilt center; press seams toward the strips.

8. Join the M/N strips on the short ends to make a long strip; press seams to one side. Subcut into two 77½" M strips and two 65½" N strips.

9. Sew the M strips to opposite long sides and the N strips to the top and bottom of the pieced center; press seams toward the strips.

10. Join the O/P strips on the short ends to make a long strip; press seams to one side. Subcut into two 79½" O strips and two 75½" P strips.

11. Sew the O strips to opposite long sides and the P strips to the top and bottom of the pieced center to complete the top; press seams toward the strips.

12. Layer, quilt and bind with the 2¼" dark blue tonal strips, following Finishing Your Quilt on page 6 in General Instructions. ❖

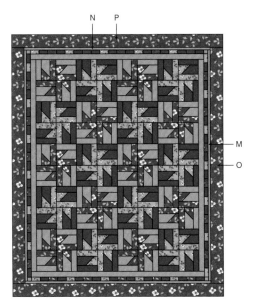

Tied With a Bow
Placement Diagram 75" x 89"

Metric Conversion Charts

Metric Conversions

Canada/U.S. Measurement		Multiplied by		Metric Measurement
yards	x	.9144	=	metres (m)
yards	x	91.44	=	centimetres (cm)
inches	x	2.54	=	centimetres (cm)
inches	x	25.40	=	millimetres (mm)
inches	x	.0254	=	metres (m)

Canada/U.S. Measurement		Multiplied by		Metric Measurement
centimetres	x	.3937	=	inches
metres	x	1.0936	=	yards

Standard Equivalents

Canada/U.S. Measurement		Metric Measurement		
⅛ inch	=	3.20 mm	=	0.32 cm
¼ inch	=	6.35 mm	=	0.635 cm
⅜ inch	=	9.50 mm	=	0.95 cm
½ inch	=	12.70 mm	=	1.27 cm
⅝ inch	=	15.90 mm	=	1.59 cm
¾ inch	=	19.10 mm	=	1.91 cm
⅞ inch	=	22.20 mm	=	2.22 cm
1 inch	=	25.40 mm	=	2.54 cm
⅛ yard	=	11.43 cm	=	0.11 m
¼ yard	=	22.86 cm	=	0.23 m
⅜ yard	=	34.29 cm	=	0.34 m
½ yard	=	45.72 cm	=	0.46 m
⅝ yard	=	57.15 cm	=	0.57 m
¾ yard	=	68.58 cm	=	0.69 m
⅞ yard	=	80.00 cm	=	0.80 m
1 yard	=	91.44 cm	=	0.91 m
1⅛ yards	=	102.87 cm	=	1.03 m
1¼ yards	=	114.30 cm	=	1.14 m

Canada/U.S. Measurement				Metric Measurement
1⅜ yards	=	125.73 cm	=	1.26 m
1½ yards	=	137.16 cm	=	1.37 m
1⅝ yards	=	148.59 cm	=	1.49 m
1¾ yards	=	160.02 cm	=	1.60 m
1⅞ yards	=	171.44 cm	=	1.71 m
2 yards	=	182.88 cm	=	1.83 m
2⅛ yards	=	194.31 cm	=	1.94 m
2¼ yards	=	205.74 cm	=	2.06 m
2⅜ yards	=	217.17 cm	=	2.17 m
2½ yards	=	228.60 cm	=	2.29 m
2⅝ yards	=	240.03 cm	=	2.40 m
2¾ yards	=	251.46 cm	=	2.51 m
2⅞ yards	=	262.88 cm	=	2.63 m
3 yards	=	274.32 cm	=	2.74 m
3⅛ yards	=	285.75 cm	=	2.86 m
3¼ yards	=	297.18 cm	=	2.97 m
3⅜ yards	=	308.61 cm	=	3.09 m
3½ yards	=	320.04 cm	=	3.20 m
3⅝ yards	=	331.47 cm	=	3.31 m
3¾ yards	=	342.90 cm	=	3.43 m
3⅞ yards	=	354.32 cm	=	3.54 m
4 yards	=	365.76 cm	=	3.66 m
4⅛ yards	=	377.19 cm	=	3.77 m
4¼ yards	=	388.62 cm	=	3.89 m
4⅜ yards	=	400.05 cm	=	4.00 m
4½ yards	=	411.48 cm	=	4.11 m
4⅝ yards	=	422.91 cm	=	4.23 m
4¾ yards	=	434.34 cm	=	4.34 m
4⅞ yards	=	445.76 cm	=	4.46 m
5 yards	=	457.20 cm	=	4.57 m

HOUSE of WHITE BIRCHES
PUBLISHERS SINCE 1947

Quilted Curves & Stripes With the AccuQuilt GO! is published by DRG, 306 E. Parr Road, Berne, IN 46711. Printed in USA. Copyright © 2011 DRG. All rights reserved. This publication may not be reproduced in part or in whole without written permission from the publisher.

RETAIL STORES: If you would like to carry this pattern book or any other DRG publications, visit DRGwholesale.com

Every effort has been made to ensure that the instructions in this pattern book are complete and accurate. We cannot, however, take responsibility for human error, typographical mistakes or variations in individual work. Please visit ClotildeCustomerCare.com to check for pattern updates.

ISBN: 978-1-59217-376-1

1 2 3 4 5 6 7 8 9

Snails' Trail

Continued from page 57

Completing the Quilt

1. Select eight blocks. Stitch blocks together to make a row matching red corners between blocks as shown in Figure 7. Press seams in one direction. Repeat to make eight rows.

Make 8

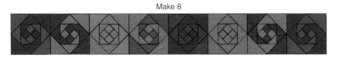

Figure 7

2. Referring to the Placement Diagram, arrange and stitch rows together so that red corners match between rows. Carefully remove the foundation paper and press seams in one direction.

3. Join C/D strips on short ends to make one long strip; press seams in one direction. Cut the C/D strip into two 56½" C borders and two 62½" D borders.

4. Sew C to opposite sides of pieced center and D to top and bottom referring to placement diagram.

5. Layer, quilt and bind with solid black 2¼" strips, following Finishing Your Quilt on page 6 in General Instructions. ❖

Special Thanks & Supplies

Thank you to AccuQuilt for providing GO!® Fabric Cutters and dies to our talented team of designers.

Page 8: Picket Fence Place Mats—Sulky® threads and Soft & Bright batting from The Warm Company.

Page 12: Tumbler Tote—Happy fabric collection from Moda and Pellon #987F fusible fleece.

Page 16: Christmas Candy Apples—O' Tinsel Tree fabric collection from Robert Kaufman, Bamboo batting from Fairfield and Star Machine Quilting thread from Coats.

Page 24: Winding Ways—Soft & Bright batting from The Warm Company and Pol-Lite Thread from Sulky®.

Page 30: Fractured Tumblers—Urban Cosmos fabric collection from Windham Fabrics, Fairfield Nature-Fil bamboo batting and Star Machine Quilting thread from Coats.

Page 38: Dancing Pinwheels—Essentials Collection from Wilmington Prints, Fairfield Nature-Fil bamboo batting and Star Machine Quilting & Craft thread from Coats.

Page 45: Roundabout—Super by Gudrun Erla for Red Rooster Fabrics.

Page 50: Scrappy Braid—Fairfield Nature-Fil bamboo batting and Star Machine Quilting Thread from Coats.

Page 59: Tied With a Bow—Gallery Fiori fabric collection by Karen Tusinski for P&B Textiles, Fairfield Nature-Fil bamboo batting and Star Machine Quilting & Craft thread from Coats.

Photo Index

8

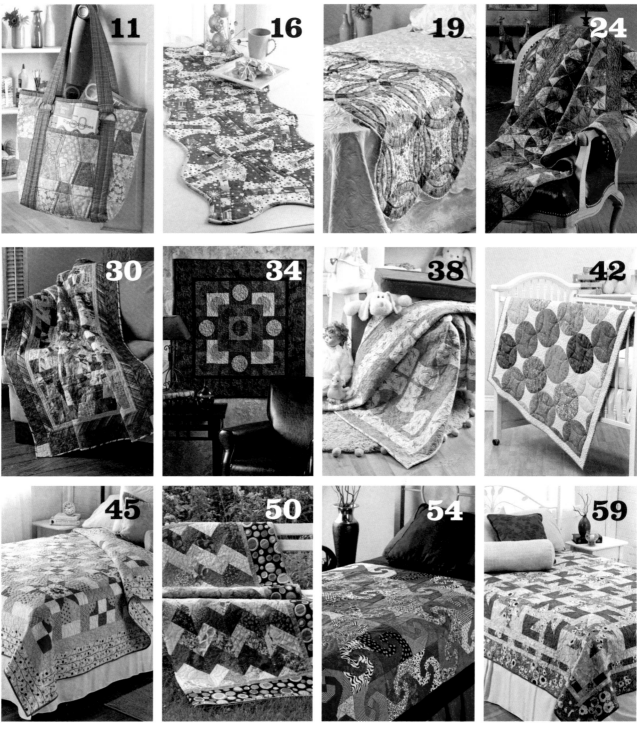

11

16

19

24

30

34

38

42

45

50

54

59